Whale Done
Parenting

Whale Done Parenting

How to Make Parenting
a Positive Experience
for You and Your Kids

Ken Blanchard
Thad Lacinak
Chuck Tompkins
Jim Ballard

BK

Berrett–Koehler Publishers, Inc.
San Francisco
a BK Life book

Berrett-Koehler Publishers, Inc.
235 Montgomery Street, Suite 650
San Francisco, CA 94104-2916
Tel: (415) 288-0260   Fax: (415) 362-2512   www.bkconnection.com

ORDERING INFORMATION

Quantity sales. Special discounts are available on quantity purchases by corporations, associations, and others. For details, contact the "Special Sales Department" at the Berrett-Koehler address above.

Individual sales. Berrett-Koehler publications are available through most bookstores. They can also be ordered directly from Berrett-Koehler: Tel: (800) 929-2929; Fax: (802) 864-7626; www.bkconnection.com

Orders for college textbook/course adoption use. Please contact Berrett-Koehler: Tel: (800) 929-2929; Fax: (802) 864-7626.

Orders by U.S. trade bookstores and wholesalers. Please contact Ingram Publisher Services, Tel: (800) 509-4887; Fax: (800) 838-1149; E-mail: customer.service @ingrampublisherservices.com; or visit www.ingrampublisherservices.com/ Ordering for details about electronic ordering.

Berrett-Koehler and the BK logo are registered trademarks of Berrett-Koehler Publishers, Inc.

Printed in the United States of America

Berrett-Koehler books are printed on long-lasting acid-free paper. When it is available, we choose paper that has been manufactured by environmentally responsible processes. These may include using trees grown in sustainable forests, incorporating recycled paper, minimizing chlorine in bleaching, or recycling the energy produced at the paper mill.

Production Management: Michael Bass Associates

Library of Congress Cataloging-in-Publication Data

Whale done parenting : how to make parenting a positive experience for you and your kids / Ken Blanchard ... [et al.].
        p. cm.
    ISBN 978-1-60509-348-2 (alk. paper)
    1. Parenting. 2. Reinforcement (Psychology) I. Blanchard, Kenneth H.
HQ755.8.W464 2009
649'.6—dc22   2009023953

First Edition
14 13 12 11 10 09   10 9 8 7 6 5 4 3 2 1

*This book is
dedicated
to
parents everywhere
who
want to make
parenting
a positive experience
for themselves
and
their kids.*

Contents

Foreword

Jim Atchison is president of Busch Entertainment Corporation, which operates 10 U.S. theme parks including Sea-World, Busch Gardens, and Discovery Cove.

WE FIRST MET Ken Blanchard seven years ago in Orlando, Florida. Ken was promoting his new book with appearances in the three Sea-World parks. The presentation he gave at Shamu Stadium that day borrowed heavily from the themes of *Whale Done! The Power of Positive Relationships*, a 2002 collaborative project between Ken, marine mammal training pioneers Chuck Tompkins and Thad Lacinak, Ken's longtime friend and colleague Jim Ballard, and SeaWorld. That book would go on to help hundreds of thousands of people establish more productive and positive relationships at home and at work.

Ken had no way of knowing that morning that Elli and I were soon to embark on life's greatest, most rewarding, and, sometimes, most frustrating adventure: We were about to start our own family. In the brief time that has passed since meeting Ken, we have had three beautiful children. Caleb is six, Nathanael is four, and Bethany is two, ages that are represented in many of the young characters in this book. We are pleased to report that every technique you're about to learn has been validated—repeatedly—in the Atchison house.

Our chat with Ken that morning in Orlando revealed that he is, at heart, a teacher—a man who reflects on his own experiences and delights in sharing them with others in ways that make life easier, more fulfilling, and more productive. After reading just one of his books, a collaboration with legendary Miami Dolphins coach Don Shula, it was clear that an association between Ken Blanchard and SeaWorld was inevitable.

As Ken likes to point out, SeaWorld does many things well, but one thing better than anyone else: caring for, training, and showcasing marine mammals. SeaWorld's sophistication in marine mammal care translates for our guests to really only one thing: fun. But it meant a great deal more to Ken. From his first visit to our San Diego SeaWorld in the '70s, he realized that training marine mammals, including large predators like killer whales, must have applications for human relationships. How could it not? A killer whale can weigh 13,000 pounds. It is the ocean's top predator. As SeaWorld trainers are fond of pointing out, a wise person *demands* nothing of a killer whale. You rely on a relationship based on mutual respect and trust, then you *ask* something of a killer whale.

All of us at SeaWorld are delighted to continue our relationship with Ken in this latest evolution of the Whale Done philosophy, *Whale Done Parenting*. We hope the lessons in this book provide meaningful insights that work as well in your home as they do in ours.

— Jim and Elli Atchison

Introduction
Redirecting Your Thinking about Parenting

AS A PARENT, have you ever had a child throw a tantrum or refuse to go to bed on time, eat good foods, or share toys? Do you find yourself scolding or yelling at your child and overusing the word *no*? Have you despaired of training your child to use the potty? Do you struggle with getting a child to do homework or chores? Do you deal with teasing, fighting, or poor manners? Do you need better methods for setting limits and handling time-outs and discipline?

Parenting can be trying. As challenges pile up, it's easy for a mom or dad to get into a rut and become locked into a negative, downward spiral that makes the relationship unpleasant for both parent and child. At such times it's difficult even to imagine that there might be a better way. But that better way is precisely what this book offers. Simply put, it's a way to feel good as a parent—good about yourself, good about your relationship with your child, and good about life at home again.

Whale Done Parenting contains a formula that is positive and based on principles that are scientifically validated. Most important of all, it works! This is a book about bringing to the parenting of children the behavioral principles that have succeeded spectacularly in marine mammal training. The principle is a familiar one: Accentuate the positive and eliminate the negative. It's actually simple, but it is anything but easy.

Much of the book focuses on children up to the age of five, but later chapters explain how the same techniques can be applied to older children, including teenagers. Indeed, the Whale Done approach works with people of all ages because it is based on universal principles of behavioral science.

Most new parents model their approach on what their own parents did. In some cases this turns out okay; more often these parents perpetuate the negative aspects of parenting they remember. The results can be disastrous. The principles and techniques presented in *Whale Done Parenting* are taken not from memories of childhood or armchair speculation, but from solid behavioral science principles.

As we described in the first book, *Whale Done!*, modern marine mammal training is based on positive reinforcement. It wasn't always so. In the early 1970s animal training was a different world. At that time, there was very little science in the approaches animal trainers used.

Animal training at that time was a male-dominated profession. In most cases, individual trainers forged their own styles and strategies with limited success and with limited attempt to cooperate or share ideas with their fellow trainers. Back then we weren't purposely ignoring the science of operant conditioning—we simply didn't know what operant conditioning was!

SeaWorld animal trainers began to think *there must be a better way.* They undertook a thorough examination of the field of behavioral science. The result was that SeaWorld was instrumental in pioneering the reinforcement-based training now used throughout the world.

We were very limited with the kinds of reinforcement that we used. The use of one reinforcer—food—was limited in its ability to develop deep, lasting relationships with the animals. Gradually SeaWorld trainers—using a wide variety of things whales liked, to reward and reinforce desired behaviors—evolved stronger bonds that eventually allowed us to get in the water with the animals. This led to the spectacular performances you see from these animals today.

As Thad and Chuck were learning about training killer whales, Ken Blanchard was observing the negative effects of command-and-control leadership on people in organizations. Ken was suggesting that the key to developing people was to catch them doing something right. Serendipity brought Thad, Chuck, Ken, and Jim together, and the result was *Whale Done! The Power of Positive Relationships.*

Since its publication in 2003 *Whale Done!* not only has achieved extraordinary success, but it also has changed lives in the process. It's a story of how a man established good relationships with his family and company by applying the same set of principles used by professionals to train killer whales. In the years since bringing out *Whale Done!* we have often been asked, "Can the principles featured in that book be applied to parenting young children?" It became very clear that a second book was needed that would provide a resounding *yes* to that query. Applying Whale Done training to children is a natural process. In fact, it's much easier and more lasting than with adults.

Whale Done is much more than a set of techniques. It is an entire philosophy, one that is sorely needed in the world today. Simply stated, what we call Whale Done is a way of looking at people and seeing the best that is in them. Our hope is that this book will educate and inspire mothers, fathers, grandparents, and others who help raise children to look at their roles with new eyes. And we trust that as you read the story of Amy and Matt and their son Josh, you will recognize what you knew all along: there's power in being positive.

CHAPTER

One

An Exciting New Job and Challenges at Home

TAKING A BREAK at SeaWorld, Amy Sheldrake
sat deep in thought by a large pool, watching several of her favorite killer whales. *How can it be possible that a whole year has passed since I came to work here?*
she thought.

"You all are some of my closest friends," Amy said
aloud. As the great gleaming black-and-white forms
moved by, their eyes lifting and their great heads nodding
at her, she imagined they understood every word she
spoke.

"Not only that, you're the best teachers I've ever had. I
can't tell you what it means to me that you've given me
such a great start as a mom. You've helped me lay the foun-
dation for all the years ahead that I'll be spending with my
son. What a difference it's made, to be here and watch how
you've responded to your trainers' kindness and consis-

5

tency. Every time you perform your incredible aerial maneuvers in the show, or ride us on your backs, or lift us high out of the water in one of your super leaps, the fans in the stands applaud in amazement. To them, it's a mystery how we trainers get you to do those things. But we know, don't we, my friends?"

Amy fell silent and spent time just watching her finny companions. She loved all the whales, whose names were derived from the Alaskan Indian culture. The name of the big whale, Kusti, meant "way of life." Sagu stood for "joy," which was fitting. Kagan meant "light." Tutan translated to "hope," and the youngest, Taat, meant "night."

Amy continued, "I've always been able to count on you guys to show me when I'm being inconsistent. You've not only taught me the Whale Done process, you've also inspired me to apply it in my role as a parent. Watching my boy Josh respond to the principles is always a thrill to me. I just hope I'll always remember what you have taught me so well!"

One year earlier . . .

Amy was sitting with her fellow trainees, Steve Gutierrez and Lorraine Ackerman, high in the stands of the aquatic park stadium.

"There's the signal for the whale to leap out of the water! Come on, Kusti!" Amy whispered eagerly.

Moments later a chorus of *oohs* and *aahs* rose from the stands as the audience responded to a spectacular leap by the eleven-thousand-pound killer whale. They watched in breathless fascination as a female trainer—whose wet-suited form had been seen moments before treading water in the center of the pool—was catapulted out of the pool on the nose of the gigantic animal as it rose suddenly and spectacularly from the blue depths below her. Up, impossibly up, went the huge glossy black-and-white form until it seemed to hang in the air, water showering down from its sides. The woman stood relaxed and poised atop the whale's nose until, at the height of the lift, she made a perfect thirty-foot dive back into the water.

"Let's hear it for Kusti and Laurie!" the announcer's voice enthused over the loudspeakers. While thunderous applause and shouts broke out from two thousand spectators around them, the three trainees grinned and gave each other high-fives.

"You called that one, Amy," Steve said admiringly.

"Yeah, Amy," said Lorraine, "nice job picking out the signal. I missed it."

Amy smiled. "Thanks," she said. "I was lucky."

The three trainers-in-training had been assigned to watch the famous SeaWorld killer whale show from the stands in order to identify the hand signals, whistle toots, and other prompts given by the trainers that cued the animals during their performances. As the show continued,

Amy and the others took notes, carefully observing the cues the show staff gave for actions by the whales. As each feat ended and the audience's attention was cleverly diverted elsewhere, the trainees observed the reinforcing techniques that the trainers surreptitiously used to reward each animal's performance.

"They are hardly using any fish," Lorraine said.

"I think it's because it's a late afternoon show," Amy replied.

"Right," Lorraine came back. "The whales have had ninety percent of their food for the day by this time. That's why we're seeing mostly tactile and some of the whales' favorite toys used today."

Amy added, "I notice them using underarm rubbing for Kusti. He likes to be massaged under his pectorals. But I found out the other day that Kagan doesn't go for that. She's strictly into back rubs."

"Look," Lorraine said, pointing to the far side of the pool as the audience watched an event at the near end. "Jared is using the water from the hose to massage Sagu's gums, to reinforce the back flip he just did. He really likes that."

"You can't have too much variety of rewards for these animals," Steve concluded.

Throughout the event, the crowd reacted with awe and delight. The show ended with the huge stars sliding out on a ramp and waving to the crowd with their huge tails, called *flukes*. As the audience began leaving the stadium, Amy overheard the familiar comments: "Those killer whales are amazing. How do they get them to *do* those things?" While the bleachers emptied around them, the trio sat comparing notes. Finally, they rose and made their way down to the pool and toward a door that led to the backstage area.

"Can you believe," said Lorraine, "that soon the three of us will be out there performing for that audience?"

"I know. It's amazing," Steve said.

"But of course," Amy reminded her peers as she opened the door, "the whales are the stars. We're along for the rides." She gestured toward the series of habitats where the huge rounded backs of five graceful killer whales were calm in the water. As she and the others moved toward the office with their notes for the debriefing session, Amy looked out at the now familiar scene. Kusti and Sagu, the two whales that had performed in the recent show, were now serene in contrast to the explosive energy and strength they had just demonstrated.

A whale named Tutan left the feeding area and swam over, eyeing Amy and lifting its huge head in greeting. The young woman felt a familiar tingle in her spine. It was the excitement of experiencing the fulfillment of a lifelong dream. From the time she was a tiny tot with a puppy named Scooter, Amy had been drawn to animals. Through the years, a succession of pets, from fish and turtles to gerbils, dogs, and cats (and one sick squirrel) occupied her home. It was when her father took her to see the dolphin movie *Flipper* that her passion for large aquatic animals was born.

In the end, it was the majestic killer whales that stole her heart. All those times sitting in the audience at the SeaWorld show, her mind had been fixed on one goal: she wanted to become a killer whale trainer. Following college, where she'd majored in behavioral psychology, she'd married Matt Sheldrake. And now there was Josh, their two-year-old son. Thinking of Josh, Amy couldn't wait to get home and see him again.

The day wore on, replete with hard work and demonstrations by coaches. On her way home, Amy had mixed feelings. On one hand was the excitement of being at SeaWorld. On the other hand, she missed Josh terribly and had concerns about leaving him. Like many youngsters his age, her son was a rambunctious child. Energetic and high-strung, he already knew how to manipulate his mom and dad. It seemed he was always pushing the limits of their control. Often their attempts at problem solving with the youngster seemed to lead nowhere. This, more than anything, was the reason Amy felt guilty starting a new career. By the time she pulled into the parking lot at Sundance Playschool she was thinking, *What kind of a mother would leave her tiny son to start a fun job as an animal trainer?* When she stopped the self-blaming and analyzed her feelings, she saw that, at bottom, she was really just missing Josh.

She hurried inside the center, noting other mothers helping their kids into their coats. Then her heart leaped as she saw Josh come running, holding out his arms and grinning. She gathered him up in her arms, and they started out the door.

"Don't forget the parent meeting tonight," the head teacher called from the office. "It's at 7:30."

That night as Amy drove home after the daycare center meeting, she was thinking over the exciting day she'd put in at SeaWorld. She couldn't wait to tell Matt all about the new things she'd learned in working with the killer whales. But as she opened the front door, her enthusiasm was stifled. Matt was sitting on the couch with his head in his hands. The place was littered with toys and other small articles. Screams and cries were coming from Josh's room.

"What happened here?" Amy asked in wonder.

"What happened?" Matt said loudly in great frustration. "What happened was *Josh!*"

"Trouble getting him to bed, huh?" Amy asked.

Matt shook his head. "The kid wore me out!"

As Amy thought back to all the times she and Matt had picked the baby up and held him when he wouldn't sleep, she realized regretfully that they had helped Josh form a bad habit. Now, at the age of two, the tyke was still acting as if Mom and Dad were at his beck and call after he'd been put to bed.

Amy and Matt looked at each other as their son's moans continued. "He's trained us well," Amy said.

Matt sighed. "That's right. I wish we could reverse it and become the trainers ourselves."

"Funny you should say that," Amy said, smiling. "I've been thinking there are some things I'm learning at Sea-World that we could use to get ourselves back into that role."

"I guess it's never too late to change," said Matt, yawning and looking at his watch. "It's late and we're tired. I say we hold a meeting tomorrow and plan our attack."

The Bedtime Waltz
Establishing a Bedtime Routine

THE NEXT MORNING at SeaWorld, the staff and the three trainees gathered at poolside for a demonstration by Clint Jordan, the park curator and head trainer. He began with a warm greeting to the three newcomers. "The staff and I want you to know you are very welcome in our training program." Cheers and whistles broke out from the group of trainers. "Each of you," Clint went on, "has survived a rigorous interview and background-checking process to ensure that you are in the right place. I needn't tell you that you are entering into a job that many people would love to have. In the entire world, only a handful get this opportunity. In fact, there are more astronauts than killer whale trainers.

"Let's talk about safety," said Clint. "There is an element of risk in working with these animals, especially with new people they don't know. Killer whales are the top predators in the ocean. Adult whales can reach lengths of eighteen to twenty-three feet and weigh up to twelve thousand pounds. We have guidelines and emergency procedures in case someone were to jump or fall into the pool with the whales. In our shows we have safety guidelines for the public and for our training staff. It's imperative that you follow instructions carefully as you get to know these animals.

"New trainers also need to learn all the behavior terminology so that communication between the trainers is consistent." Clint held up the whistle he wore around his neck. "For instance, the whistle is used to tell the whales *yes* when they've performed a particular behavior correctly. We speak of the whistle as a *bridging stimulus* because it bridges the time from when the animal does the correct behavior to the time the whale receives the reward such as fish, a rubdown, or a whale toy. Now I'd like to have you watch Jody demonstrate some maneuvers with her friend Kagan."

Jody, an experienced trainer Amy had watched many times in the shows, stepped to the pool edge. She gave a quick hand signal, and a giant form was suddenly racing through the water and gliding to a stop at her feet. For the next few minutes Jody put Kagan through a series of drills, carefully rewarding the animal after each performance of the desired action. From the looks on their faces, Amy saw that the trainees were in awe. Watching Kagan flawlessly obey the signals, they undoubtedly were wondering how the training of the whale had been carried out. They were about to learn the answer.

As Jody gave Kagan an appreciative rubdown, Clint again took center stage. "There are three basic rules of animal training that we try to follow at all times." He gestured to a sign on the wall by the pool that listed three steps:

1. *Set the animal up for success.*

2. *Ignore failure and/or redirect.*

3. *Reward success.*

Pointing to the first rule, he said, "Part of setting Kagan up for success was learning her habits, her past history, her likes and dislikes, what part of the day she has the most energy, which trainer she responds best to, and so on. Setting up for success includes eliminating any reinforcement for doing an undesirable behavior."

Pointing to rule 2, Clint commented, "You don't regard failure as a bad thing. You try to call the least amount of attention to a behavior you don't want, so as not to reinforce it. Meanwhile, you look out for success, and when it comes, you jump up and down and reinforce it like crazy.

"That leads us to rule 3," Clint continued. "Success isn't just reaching the finish line—it's in a number of small approximations, each of which needs to be observed and rewarded. In as many ways as you can, you make the animal feel good about what it's done, even if it's just a slight movement toward the target. Food, play time, toys, rubdowns—you make sure that this whale is going to associate all those good feelings with doing it right."

That evening, Amy couldn't wait to share with Matt what she had learned and see how they could apply this knowledge to Josh's bedtime issue. "Clint Jordan, our head trainer, gave us a talk today about the basics of whale training," she said. "He calls it the Whale Done method." Amy told Matt about the three basic rules of training— setting up for success, ignoring failure/redirecting, and rewarding success.

"I've been thinking about the first rule and what we might do differently to *set Josh up for success*," Amy continued. "One idea I have is to limit his naps, so he's sleepy in the evening. I could talk to the teachers at his day care center about keeping him more alert. If I explain why, I'm sure they'll cooperate."

Matt nodded. "Sounds good."

"We could also make sure that evening activities are quiet. No TV blaring. No running around or rambunctious play, like you and Josh have been doing," Amy continued.

Matt frowned. "I don't think the Hulk is going to appreciate us canceling wrestling matches where he defeats all opponents."

"You mean *you're* not going to appreciate it!" Amy chided.

Matt smiled. "On the other hand, if the Hulk and I moved our match to the early part of the evening, he would be worn out later on. Then, as you say, the later part of the evening could be calmer. I could read him a quiet story."

Amy nodded approvingly. "That covers the first rule for now," she said. "Let's talk about the second rule, *ignoring failure*. This, to me, is one of the biggest learnings I'm having at work. I'm in awe of the patience and persistence those trainers have in bringing the least amount of attention to what the animals do wrong. How do you think that rule might play out for us in this going-to-bed issue?"

Matt thought for a while. "Ignoring failure will be a real change for me. I guess you'd say I was 'calling attention' to our boy's not going to bed the other night! But if you and I do all we can to make sure he's sleepy and peaceful, we don't have to make a big fuss if he still doesn't cooperate. Just leave him in bed if he hollers and stay calm ourselves."

"And make no reference to his negative times," Amy added.

"Okay, good, so we ignore failure," Matt said. "The third rule says *reward success*. How does that work? Does it mean we make a big deal the next morning after he's gone to bed with no fuss?"

"Absolutely," Amy replied, "especially at first. We don't miss a single chance to recognize even the slightest improvement in Josh's cooperation about going to bed. This is the most powerful strategy of all. The first two rules just prepare the way for him to do something right, so we can be all over him with hugs and surprises and other things he likes. Whenever Josh goes to bed without a fuss, we make him feel really good in every way we can."

Matt shrugged. "Have to admit, it makes sense."

Amy's eyes lit up. "It's like what Clint told us today," she said. "Success isn't just reaching the finish line—it's in a number of small steps, and each step needs to be observed and rewarded. The idea is to make the animal feel good about what it's done, even if it's just moving toward the target. So success doesn't have to be perfect. We can reward in increments."

"So if Josh is good about going to bed," Matt chimed in, "we don't have to wait until morning to reward him. Each time I put him in his crib and he's peaceful, I can say, 'Daddy's proud of you for going to bed so nicely and quietly. That's really helpful to Mommy and Daddy!'"

Amy laughed. "You are really getting it, Mr. Behaviorist."

"It's worth a try," Matt said, "since nothing else we've done so far has worked!"

That evening Amy and Matt carried out each step of their plan. Nevertheless, Josh made his usual protest at bedtime. As the couple sat down in the living room, listening to the cries coming from the bedroom, Amy said, "Josh was looking sleepy this afternoon when I picked him up, so I played a game with him when we got home. He's got to be pretty tired by now, though he's fighting it.

"At SeaWorld they stress the importance of communication, so earlier today I talked to Josh about bedtime. I was very calm and picked my times when he was playing happily. I said things like, 'It's going to be fun to go to bed tonight.' Once I took him to his crib where his stuffed toys are, I said, 'Poodles and Ralph are going to be so happy to see Josh coming to sleep with them.'"

Matt nodded. "We did it all—keeping him up fairly late, making sure to eliminate any noise or strenuous activities close to bedtime." He smiled. "Then I read him his favorite story. It felt good to have him snuggling up to me."

"That bonding time is probably most important," Amy said. "When I put him in I made sure he had his friends close to him. One thing I've learned in working with the killer whales is that routines are good, but they shouldn't be too rigid. We want predictability with Josh, but we also need to vary the routine so we don't create expectations that he's going to insist on."

"I get it," Matt said. "We shouldn't always have story time be exactly fifteen minutes long. And maybe we should substitute something else for story time once in a while."

"That's it," Amy agreed.

They listened again as Josh's sounds turned to drowsy moans, then subsided to whimpers.

Matt sighed. "We haven't gone in there once. What a change from the battles we used to have! I always dreaded his bedtime, but even this first night of the new plan, I feel more in control."

"Don't forget the all-important third rule when he cooperates," Amy said. "We'll need to call attention to anything he does toward the goal of going to bed and to sleep on his own, and make a big deal about it."

Matt grinned. "I'm not going to go in there as soon as he's asleep, wake him up, and say, 'Nice job, kid.'"

Amy laughed. "No, I mean in the evenings ahead, as we keep this up, we'll need to be on our toes to praise progress. And in the times Josh really goes to bed well, we should be in there first thing the next morning telling him we're proud of him for it."

"I'm beginning to see why this stuff you're learning works," Matt said thoughtfully. "What hits me is how common it is for parents to do the thing exactly *backward*— to call attention to the bad stuff and ignore the good stuff. I think what we unknowingly do by those responses is train kids, employees, and even each other to do the wrong thing!"

Each evening after that, Amy and Matt continued to follow their routine to help reshape Josh's bedtime behavior. They began to see progress and were careful to celebrate each instance of it. After two weeks, Josh was making hardly any fuss about going to bed. Clearly, the hour before bedtime had become his family time, and he was enjoying being the star.

During the training period, Amy was able to arrange with Josh's day care teacher to keep him alert during nap time by allowing him some special quiet activity. It seemed the parents were covering all the bases—with one exception.

Since he was an infant, Josh had insisted that his mother be the one to tuck him in each evening. One evening Amy had to be away late attending a meeting, and it was clearly Matt's night to solo. All went well until story time ended and Matt indicated that he and Josh were headed for the bedroom. That's when the howling and fussing began. Later, when Amy returned, she found Matt exhausted and a great wailing coming from Josh's room.

"I've practically had to tie myself to the couch to keep from going in there," Matt said.

For the next several nights, both Amy and Matt put their son to bed for a few nights. Then they began to alternate. Soon it didn't matter so much who did the tucking in.

Later, when bedtime had become fun time, Amy was able one night to say to Josh, "I'll bet you could pick up all your toys before sleep time!" To his mother's delight, Josh hurried around, collecting toys and putting them away. Amy rewarded each put-away by laughing and applauding.

"Now, you're so sleepy you're ready for bed," she said when the job was done. With much praising and reward- ing, this cleaning up soon became a bedtime ritual.

One evening the parents were talking about their new regimes with Josh. "Seems like you have to build backward if you started out the wrong way," Matt said one evening.

"That's right," Amy agreed. "And playing catch-up as parents is okay, as long as we know where we're going."

"Even with these Whale Done ways," Matt said worriedly, "things seem to take longer that I expect them to." He sighed. "Do you suppose we're, you know, *behind* some parents? Is our kid . . . you know . . . *normal* in the time he takes to learn these basic things?" Then he quickly added, "It's stupid to worry about these things, huh?"

Amy smiled and patted her husband's arm. "Not so much. In fact, I asked the head trainer at work about those same concerns. His answer was, 'Worry not. Compare not. Normal is what's normal for Josh.'"

BEDTIME

Set things up for success

Establishing a bedtime routine is an effective way to calm and help your child transition from activities of the day to the quiet of the night. The routine should move from active to passive; noisy to quiet. Add a warm bath, soft music, or a special going-to-bed song, and a small glass of water so thirst is not a reason to get up. Above all, make going to bed fun. Keep the event the same, but vary its length and frequency, and make it appropriate to your child's likes and dislikes. If your child naps, make the nap early.

Ignore failure and/or redirect

Avoid calling attention to the negative by *redirecting*—putting attention on something for which you can praise your child. The redirection you choose must be easily doable, developmentally appropriate, and based on your child's preferences. A warm bath is a good part of the bedtime routine. If your child is hesitant, dip his hand in the water, then a foot, until he is immersed and realizing it is fun. If your child refuses to take a bath, do necessary cleaning with a washcloth, and then take one of your child's toys and start washing it in the tub, saying how nice the toy feels to be so clean. Invite your child to participate, and praise him for the help. Another example: Ask your child to dim the light in the bedroom. If he refuses, pretend to show a teddy bear how the light goes up and down in brightness. ("See, how fun this is!")

Give a Whale Done!

Reward every evidence of your child's interest, attention, or participation. For instance, when your child helps to bathe the toy, reward him with praise or a hug. When he contributes an idea or helps with establishing the going-to-bed routine, reinforce each such attitude with a Whale Done. If appropriate, keep a chart of bedtimes and wake-up times. Highlight those times that indicate success and celebrate them. When your child sleeps all night, make a big deal of it.

CHAPTER
Three

A-B-C
The Universal Principle

AMY ARRIVED at work the following week eager to learn more, as the head trainer, Clint, would be speaking to the trainees again. She spent the morning learning from Jody about the very important matter of the whales' diet.

As they went about distributing the buckets of fish, Amy said, "I imagine the water temperature is pretty much the same as the ocean would be."

Jody smiled. "Fifty-two degrees," she said. "When you get in there, even with a wetsuit, you know it!"

By the time noon rolled around, Amy was glad to sit down with the other trainees for an order-out lunch. As they ate, Clint came out.

"One thing we're kind of nuts about here at the park," Clint said, "is the importance of *feedback*. Most human beings don't go out of their way to provide feedback. When was the last time someone said to you, 'Hey, I notice you're doing something that way. Have you ever tried doing it *this* way?' On most jobs, people are left pretty much alone when they do things right. The only time they hear about their performance is at some annual or semiannual review. Meanwhile, if they get any feedback at all it's what we call a *gotcha* response—somebody caught them doing something wrong.

"Here, it's just the opposite. Feedback is going on all the time, between people and animals, and between people and people—and it's all constructive. The feedback you get here is not to catch you doing things wrong but to catch you doing things *right*. It's designed to help you improve and be a successful trainer. And when there is an error or failure, the feedback will simply *redirect* your behavior into the right channel."

With that, Clint introduced each of the trainers sitting in the back. "This is Jared, that's Kim Lee, and she's Brenda. These folks are experienced trainers. One of them will be assigned to each of you as your coach. This person will stay with you and oversee your progress, making sure your learning and adjusting to stay on track. After a while, we'll switch off so you can be exposed to a variety of viewpoints and experience."

As Amy watched the smiling trainers in their black wetsuits, looking so capable and professional, she knew she would be happy to be assigned to any one of them.

After all, some of these were the people she'd watched in shows from her seat in the audience, the ones who had been her idols for a decade.

As the coaches walked out with their assigned trainees, Amy found herself with Kim Lee, who smiled at her in reassurance. She noted that Steve was assigned to Jared and Brenda was to be Lorraine's coach. The pairs split up and moved around the pool area, the coaches pointing out things to their charges.

As Kim Lee and Amy made their way to a far pool, the coach made a hand signal, and one of the enormous killer whales swam immediately over to their side of the pool. Amy marveled at the animal's response.

"Meet my friend Tutan," Kim Lee said, kneeling down to stroke the whale's head and crooning at it just as if it were her own baby. Her loving admiration of the animal was evident. "Say hello to Amy, Tutan," she said, and Tutan lifted his huge head and nodded toward Amy, as if it were a handshake.

As they walked around the pool, Amy said, "I noticed the hand movement you used to cue Tutan to nod to me. It worked like clockwork. How long does it take to train each whale to do a trick like that?"

Kim Lee turned to her, smiling. "You were sharp to observe that. You'll want to keep using those good observation skills when working with the animals here. But let me redirect one thing you said. You called what I did a trick. When people see a killer whale perform one of these actions, they call it a trick, but I want *you* to be clear we're not tricking people or animals here. We're looking at specific behaviors we want to reward."

Amy reflected that she was being introduced to a kind of thinking and perceiving that was at once foreign and familiar; simple and profound. When these things had been presented in her graduate psychology classes, she'd wondered what they had to do with the real world. Here at Sea-World they were coming to life as practical strategies.

Kim Lee said, "It does take a long time to train a whale to nod like that, but most of that time is spent developing trust. Along the way failures are ignored, while each step toward success is rewarded and reinforced. Again, this is just good science." She paused a moment, then said, "In the long run, two things keep you going in this work: *patience* and *persistence*. You have to practice patience again and again, not rushing things or allowing yourself to get the slightest bit upset. And when patience is in short supply, that's when persistence kicks in."

In one of the theory sessions that afternoon, Clint Jordan introduced a new concept by writing the following on a whiteboard:

A = Activator

B = Behavior

C = Consequence

Clint explained, "This is a way of thinking about the plan we use to shape the animals' behavior. *A* stands for *activator*, that's whatever we do to set up the desired behavior to happen. *B* stands for the *behavior* we want. And *C* stands for *consequence*—what happens afterward. Which of these steps do you think is the most important?"

Steve said, "I would think it's A, because you've got to set up the animal for success and cue it with the hand signal."

"Good," Clint said. "That's definitely important, but not as important as another step."

"Gotta be B, behavior," Lorraine burst out confidently. "After all, that's what you're trying to produce."

"Sure," Clint said. "Still not the most important."

Everyone looked at Amy as if it was her turn. "Uh, C for consequence?" she said sheepishly.

"How'd you figure that out?" Clint deadpanned, and everyone laughed. "But now, why is that so? When so much time goes into training the behavior to happen, why is what you do *after it happens* the important piece?"

"Because that's the reward," Amy said, "which the animal comes to associate with doing the behavior, and therefore it's motivated to do it. The positive consequence is what drives and maintains the behavior."

"Exactly right," said Clint. "When you apply this to people at work, you find it's not so much in evidence. When they do what they're supposed to do, nobody notices. Often it's only when they mess up that a lot of fuss is made about it. Meanwhile, they're expected to carry on and do well without feedback. Have you found this to be true?"

Heads nodded, and several examples were given. Amy thought back to several jobs she'd had, where this pattern had been played out.

"No wonder people aren't motivated to go beyond what's expected in their work," said Steve. "No one seems to care."

"That's why we pay so *little* attention around here to what animals and people do *in*correctly," Clint said, "and so *much* attention to what they do *right*. I'm of the opinion that if all you did in dealing with family, friends, and even casual acquaintances was to notice and comment on what they did right, you'd find yourself among some very happy people. And you'd be pretty happy yourself, because of the way they treated you back."

As she pondered the A-B-C principle throughout the morning, Amy found herself thinking about Lorraine, her fellow trainee. From the beginning it seemed to Amy that Lorraine didn't like her, but she didn't know why. *With that sour expression,* Amy told herself, *she probably doesn't get along with anybody in her life.*

Listening to Clint's point about ignoring the negative and emphasizing the positive, Amy looked at her own tendency to judge Lorraine. *She and I are probably going to be working together here for a long time,* she thought. *It can't hurt to try this principle on her. I'm going to go out of my way to be nice to her. If she puts others off like she has me, she probably doesn't get that kind of response often.* She decided to look for something Lorraine did well and call attention to it.

At lunchtime she had her chance. Lorraine usually avoided sitting across the picnic table from Amy, but today that was the only seat not taken. After the usual lively discussion over sandwiches and soft drinks, the others drifted away. Because Lorraine's order had arrived late, she remained to finish her lunch, continuing to avoid eye contact.

"I've been meaning to tell you," Amy said, "some of your questions and comments have been really helpful to me."

Lorraine looked up suspiciously. "Really?" she said with a frown.

"Really. Your question today about the nutritional ingredients in the fish we feed the whales opened up that whole discussion about calories, and then the points about environmental changes in the oceans came out. I was fascinated. I'm one of those people who always reads food labels, but I just hadn't thought about it with regard to the whales."

Lorraine looked away and said, "That's interesting."

"Where did you learn that stuff, anyway?" Amy persisted. She found herself not only determined to meet the challenge of Lorraine's attitude but genuinely interested in the woman.

"I was a chem major in college and worked a couple of years in a hospital dietary lab."

"So was that part of the path that led you here?"

Lorraine sighed. But she evidently decided that Amy was not to be dismissed. She turned to Amy and went on with her story.

As Amy nodded and smiled and asked questions, she observed that Lorraine was starting to lose some of her reserve. Soon the call came to assemble for an animal training observation. As they rose and walked away together, Lorraine said dutifully, "Sometime you must tell me about *your* background."

Amy thought, *She's a tough cookie. Maybe she never had a mother that listened to her. But that wasn't so hard. I'll keep trying, if only to prove to myself that this A-B-C stuff works, whether on animals or humans.*

USING THE METHOD WITH PEERS

Set things up for success

Whale Done techniques work with people of all ages. That's because all of us are motivated by attention, approval, and acceptance. As shown in the book *Whale Done!*, positive responses are particularly powerful in workplace relationships, where interactions are supposedly based on rational, nonemotional thinking and behavior. People's inability to get along and communicate well are commonly cited as causes of nonproductivity and low morale. Managers who treat their people in a Whale Done way are helping build the trust, cooperation, and commitment of their people. Looking for and acknowledging what is good and acceptable in workmates' behaviors helps create a positive team environment. Mutual ignoring of faults and rewarding of right behavior can also be the basis of a strong marriage.

Ignore failure and/or redirect

Whenever you observe a behavior that is unacceptable to you, consider whether ignoring it rather than calling attention to it will enhance the relationship. When this is plainly not going to work, take the burden of blame on yourself ("Maybe I didn't make it clear what I meant; let's go over this again"). Explain what good performance looks like. Look for an outcome that can include a Whale Done for the person. When someone is upset, don't attempt to communicate logically. Retire from the scene until emotions have cooled. Later, if it makes sense, bring up the matter calmly and invite the other person's solutions. When emphasizing an idea or soliciting a particular response from another, be sure to include "what's in it for them."

Give a Whale Done!

In parenting, teaching, coaching, or managing, the most common response to good performance is no response: "She's just doing her job." "That's what they get paid for." It's easy to call attention to mistakes and errors—and much harder to notice what people do well. One Whale Done response—calling attention to right behavior—can go far toward establishing trust and a desire to do well. Perhaps this is because it is so unusual to receive a praising or a pat on the back. More likely, it's because all of us really want to do well, hunger for attention, and are motivated to do better by recognition of our best.

CHAPTER

Four

The Redirection Strategy
Handling Tantrums

"**D**ARN IT, Tutan's just not getting it."

It was a hot afternoon, and Amy was discouraged after unsuccessfully trying to get one of the younger killer whales to avoid the gate that led to the performance stadium. Each time the other animals were called there to go out into the show area and perform, Tutan would dash over there. Amy walked over to the office and found Kim Lee, her coach.

"Hey, is it just me, or is Tutan a slow learner?" she said.

"What's going on?" Kim Lee asked.

When Amy told her, she smiled. "Tutan's just excited when he sees any of his friends called to the gate. He knows something really fun is happening out there in the stadium."

Kim Lee's patient, understanding tone restored Amy's shattered confidence. She realized she hadn't been approaching the situation from Tutan's point of view. "So, what's the answer?" she asked.

"When a killer whale's acting up like this, what's the rule?" Kim prodded.

Amy took a deep breath and thought. "Look around for the reason?" she said.

"Sounds good. In this case, the whale is going to the gate because he knows the pool beyond the gate is highly reinforcing, and the other whales are going to get to go while he has to stay in back. So next time, what could you do to make him want to stay in the back pool?"

Suddenly things clicked into place in Amy's mind. "Aha," she said. "Make staying there just as rewarding as it is in the pool beyond the gate."

Kim Lee grinned and gave a thumb's up. "Rewarding good behavior is the key to so much!" she said. "Unless you stay tuned in, it's easy to miss it when those little windows of opportunity open up."

As before, it wasn't long before Amy was able to use her killer whale trainer skills at home. Her sister, Sharon, was visiting one afternoon with her two-year-old daughter, Pattie. Pattie and Josh had been playing quietly on the sun porch when suddenly Josh could be heard shouting angrily. Pattie was holding one of his toys away from him, and his arms were too short to reach it. His face was fiery red as he screamed, "Mine! Mine!"

"Pattie, don't hold that away from him," Sharon ordered. "Give it to him. It's his toy." Pattie held the toy closer, and Josh grabbed it.

Amy intervened. Getting down on one knee to be at eye level with her son, she said, "Josh, don't you know that it's okay to share your toy with your friend?" Josh looked at his toy. Then he looked at Pattie doubtfully. Then he smiled and handed it to her.

"Oh, honey, that's so good!" Amy exclaimed, and she hugged him. She stood up and took Josh over to a chart that was posted on the wall, low enough to be at the boy's eye level. Taking a box from a nearby shelf, she opened it, showing him a set of Whale Done stickers. "You get to pick one, honey," she told Josh. When he had done so, she had him place it on the chart. "That's for being a great sharer," she said.

Later, while the tots were finishing their lunch—having completely forgotten their spat—Sharon asked, "How were you able to pull that off?"

"First of all, by planning ahead," Amy said, smiling. "Matt and I started the chart once when Josh was throwing a tantrum. I don't know whether you noticed, but I waited until Josh had quieted down before I turned his attention to the chart. Unless you're careful with your timing, it's easy to reward a negative behavior unwittingly."

"But I mean, it was so immediate," Sharon said.

"Yes, it's called *redirection*, and we use it with the whales. The rule is, pay no attention to the behavior you don't want, but redirect the kid's attention to something else that's positive."

Amy looked up to see that the children were finished. As she removed their bibs, she said, "You kids did such a good job of keeping the mess off the table." She turned to her sister and said, "Then, whenever you can, throw in some praise for something they did right."

On an evening the following week, Matt and Amy were shopping at the local video store, where their attention was drawn to a young couple with a boy Josh's age. The trio was approaching the checkout counter where racks of candy were arranged strategically at small children's eye level. The youngster immediately made a move for a chocolate sucker. "No," the father pronounced.

"Oh, let him have it," the mother said. Matt's and Amy's eyes met as if to say, "This should be interesting." Realizing his advantage, the little boy set up a howl. The mom grabbed the sucker and shoved it in the child's mouth to shush him. The scenario was not finished yet, for at this point the boy dropped the sticky sucker. The father picked it up and threw it away. The boy really began to scream. Looking embarrassed, the dad picked up a new sucker and gave it to the boy. The tantrum had worked.

On the way home, Amy said, "We couldn't have found a better example of reinforcement for the wrong thing if we'd looked all night."

"Seemed like the critical point was when the mom said to let him have the sucker," Matt said. "I could see right into that kid's mind. He was saying 'I've got 'em now!'"

"Exactly right," said Amy. "The mom reinforced her son's crying. You can bet his little brain has filed that away. Kids are smart. He knows he can get his way again by causing a ruckus in public."

Matt said, "What *should* those parents have done?"

Amy thought a moment. "I'd say the scene could have been avoided when the boy picked up the candy. The dad or mom could have taken it out of his hands, gotten down on his level, and said in a quiet, reasonable way, 'When you do that, you get nothing. But if you *ask* Mommy or Daddy for what you want, you might get it.' That leaves the child a choice, and if he asks for it then and there, the candy can be the reward for following through with the right behavior. On the other hand, if he just starts to cry, they should ignore him and go about their business in the store. If he gets no attention, he'll stop. The moment he does, Mom needs to come back and say, 'Now, isn't that better? And good for you—you stopped crying all by yourself.'"

Matt said, "I think I get what you're saying. Parents should ask themselves what behavior they're rewarding when they give a child attention or a reward—even if they're in public."

"That's right," said Amy. "What's important is the immediacy of the reinforcement."

Matt drove on a while in thought. Finally, he said, "Ever have a killer whale pitch a fit like that?"

"Yes, and that case is different, because these are large, powerful animals. Main thing is just clear the area. In the process, we're giving no reinforcement to the behavior we don't want."

"I'm beginning to see some consistency in all this," Matt said. "All this causes me to reinforce a right behavior on my part."

"What's that?" Amy asked.

"You're smart, and so am I. I married above myself!"

TANTRUMS

Set things up for success

If possible, take your child to an environment that is stimulus-free (no toys, games, food, or other items that can grab attention). This permits your child to calm herself down. As soon as she is calm, reinforce the calmness. If a public upset has happened before, the next time before entering the store or other stimulating environment, explain calmly to your child the exact behavior that you want; perhaps sometimes include the promise of a reward for good behavior.

Ignore failure and/or redirect

Never try to communicate logic to a child who is in the middle of a screaming fit; it just doesn't work. Letting your child scream is all right as long as she is safe. Do not prolong the tantrum by rewarding it with attention. Ignored, the temper will dissipate by itself. Wait until your child calms down before speaking. Then you can say, "Now, don't you feel better?" When things are peaceful, say, "I want to talk with you about what happened." In explaining the behavior you want, emphasize what's in it for your child. If your child is too young to understand, communicate through your actions: ignoring the behavior you don't want, giving lots of attention to the one you do.

Give a Whale Done!

If your child has been upset before in some situation and is not upset this time, be sure to call attention to the change and reward it. If in the store situation your child puts a toy or food item back on her own, praise her, and even offer her the treat as a reward. There is nothing more rewarding, for both parent and child, than surprising your child with a reward or special celebration for good behavior. The delight of the unexpected is in itself reinforcing. It's important not to use the same reward all the time; it could eventually lose its reinforcing value. Remember: you are always trying to call to your child's attention the things she does correctly—that is, to "catch her doing things right."

An Acquired Taste
Mealtime

AFTER A LONG morning of working with the whales, Amy and her coworkers were listening to another of Clint Jordan's pep talks. "We're very careful about first impressions here," he said. "We pay lots of attention to what we call *core memory*, meaning that we want the whales to have a positive experience from the get-go, particularly when we're starting out to train a new behavior. And that goes for you folks as well. We want you to associate only good feelings with working here.

"When people start new jobs, they're usually asked to observe, but here we're kind of crazy about the matter of observation. As in all scientific inquiry, careful observation is one of the ingredients of success in working with killer whales—or any animal. Watching and mentally recording what you see is a skill that will place you ahead

of those who rely merely on hearsay or traditional thinking or who carelessly work from assumptions. Your
biggest task in getting to know these animals will be to
earn their trust. Painstaking observation will give you an
edge with them, because they'll sense right away how
responsive you are to their ways, their habits, and the dif-
ferences in their preferences.

"So *observe!* Keep your eyes open around here. How
do the whales relate to each other? What are the whales
doing when they are not being trained? What are they
doing with each other? Which whales hang out with each
other?

"Observing the animals is the key to so much we do,"
Clint continued. "For example, one of the most important reinforcing things that we use with the whales is tactile. We started doing rubs when we observed the whales
rubbing on the pool sides and each other. Now tactile
rewards can be one of the most important ones we give
the whales."

After lunch, Amy and Kim Lee were preparing the
fish buckets for feeding the whales when they noticed
that the new shipment included squid. "This was ordered
for dietary reasons," Kim Lee said. "Just like kids, the
whales are probably not going to go for it because of the
difference in texture and taste."

"What do we do, then?" Amy said.

"We'll work a training session and teach Sagu to
accept taking the squid," Kim Lee replied. "Ask Sagu to
swim over here."

Amy called Sagu over by splashing the side of the pool. Kim Lee had set up two buckets, one with Sagu's favorite fish and the other with squid. She started feeding the whale the food he was used to. While he was swallowing it, she slipped a squid in with the other fish and dropped it in when he opened his mouth. While the squid was on the way down, she offered Sagu more of the familiar fish he liked. She kept alternating the buckets this way, and finished by feeding the whale only from the fish bucket.

"Now, didn't he do well?" Kim Lee said. Amy agreed, and both began giving Sagu a good rubdown as a reward.

"*Rrrrrrrrrrrrr!* Here comes a cargo airplane preparing to land!" Matt was aiming a spoon with a pea on it at Josh's mouth. Unfortunately, the hangar doors were shut tightly while the aircraft was still circling. Moreover, Josh was shaking his head vigorously.

Matt looked helplessly across the table at Amy. "You're smiling," he said, putting the spoon down. "I'll just bet you've got a SeaWorld story for this very situation."

"Funny you should say that," Amy said. "It brings up something I learned just the other day." She told Matt about the technique she and Kim Lee had used with Sagu.

"Will it work in the long run?" Matt asked.

Amy nodded. "The very next day I was able to feed Sagu most of a half-bucket of squid, mixed with a little less fish. I was careful to reward that, too. Pretty soon he and the others we do this routine with will be eating squid independently of the fish treat."

Josh started playfully banging his spoon on his high-chair tray.

"Hold on, my man," said Matt. He turned to Amy. "So what's the plan? How are we going to get these peas into this boy's stomach?"

"We need something he likes," said Amy, thinking of the method she and Kim Lee had used with Sagu. "But we shouldn't change now to something he likes. That would be letting Josh dictate the change by not eating. We don't want to reward poor behavior."

"Okay, then, next time," Matt agreed. "What's some favorite food of his we can use to slip some peas to him? Wait—I know."

"*Mac and cheese!*" both parents chanted together.

"We'll start with the treat and add a pea," said Amy. "Then start switching and substituting back and forth. When Josh eats a pea without the macaroni, we'll make a big deal about it and then stop asking him to eat the peas."

"In other words, don't push it," said Matt.

"Right. Wait until another meal and work on it again. Praise progress, but don't try to fix the whole problem in one session or meal. If we take small steps, we'll eventually get there."

The next evening when dinner time came, Amy had the favored casserole heating up. When she brought a dishful to the table, Josh's eyes lit up. The parents followed their plan, and it worked.

"Yay, Josh!" Mom and Dad cheered.

After giving his son a hug, Matt said, "You know, Josh might not grow up liking to eat what we want him to eat."

"It's no different than with the whales," Amy replied. "The point is not to get him to like these foods. It's to get him to *eat* them. If he gets used to them, one day he's likely to choose them on his own."

After Josh was in bed, Amy said to Matt, "One of the most interesting things I'm learning from the whales about the all-important response to the behavior—the consequence—is the importance of *variable reinforcement.*"

"Uh, could you spell that out in plain English for me, honey?" Matt asked.

Amy grinned. "It means that the ways we *reinforce* Josh's good behavior—that is, the ways we reward or recognize what he does right—need to be constantly *varied.* Clint was telling us that when he first came on board, the standard way to show the killer whales they'd performed the right behavior was food. After a while, with a fish treat being the standard operating procedure, the animals were less responsive. They liked the treats, but the reward itself had lost its potency when it became the same old expected response. They found that the whales' interest perked up when the rewards were varied. Clint said that when the trainers added rubdowns, play times, new toys, and other rewards to the fish treats, and constantly mixed up the order in which they were given, the whales showed more alertness—even more creativity in their performance. When the animals didn't know what was coming next, they had more energy and aliveness."

"It sure makes sense to continually surprise the whales when rewarding them for doing the right thing," said Matt. "So, applying that principle to Josh, we need to use—what did you call it?"

"Variable reinforcement," Amy repeated.

"Right. We need to use . . . what you said . . . in working with Josh."

During the next several days, the couple compiled a variety of Whale Dones they could give to their son. They started by brainstorming the many ways they could use verbal reinforcement:

"I'm so proud of you, Josh."
"Look what you did! You [got undressed all by your-self]."
"Good for you, honey!"
"Do you know how this helps Mommy?"
"When you [eat all your vegetables], it makes me happy."
"I'm going to tell Daddy what you did so well."
"I like the way you [are being gentle with your friend]."
"It makes me so happy when you [use the potty]."

"You deserve [an extra chapter of our bedtime story]
for [saying please]."
"Josh is a [putting-toys-away] champ!"

They improved the Whale Done sticker chart. They
filled a basket with little trinkets of the sort that Josh
liked. Amy made a grab bag her son could reach into,
which included dried fruits and other treats. Soon they
had created a Whale Done tool kit of items. By following through on their plan to change the rewards continuously, each time they responded to a positive behavior
of Josh's, he never knew what was coming. One time his
cleaning up his plate would be followed by a verbal praising; later when he was told it was bedtime and cooper-
ated willingly, he got to enjoy a short original tale,
starring himself, when he was in bed.

MEALTIME

Set things up for success

Mealtime should be fun, but it can be a headache when a child is resistant to some food the parent rightly wants included in the diet. Start with a plan for making the experience enjoyable, then get creative! Be sure your child is hungry (don't give him snacks or milk just before mealtime). Camouflaging new foods is okay, but never use dessert items to tempt a child for meal items. You can make dessert the reward for eating all that is presented at that meal. Again, don't expect it to happen all at once. Take small steps and praise the progress.

Ignore failure and/or redirect

If your child spits food out, find another way. (For example, in introducing Josh to peas, the next mealtime after such an episode, Amy might have purchased the peas in pods and had Josh help her shell them, building interest in the food.) If possible, explain to your child the fun of having many, rather than few, items on the menu. Introduce each new food in a special way, knowing that you are helping your child become accustomed to a life-long acceptance of a healthy, well-rounded diet. Also, be aware that your own mealtime behavior can communicate louder than words. Avoid sending the message "Don't eat what I eat; eat what I say!"

Give a Whale Done!

Always make a fuss whenever your child includes a new food or overcomes an aversion to something. Notice and reward even small steps or approximate successes. Often parents use food as reward or reinforcement for good behavior, but children can come to expect these things every time they act in a desirable manner. Varying rewards is important—from verbal praisings, to treats, to toys, to special privileges, and so on. A Whale Done sticker chart works well, as does an extra story at bedtime or a grab bag with pencils, stickers, and other trinkets. When your child performs well in some area for a week, he gets to pull out a prize.

CHAPTER

Six

Chucking the Binky
Ending Dependency on Comfort Items

I T WAS SATURDAY and Amy had to work, so she
and Matt decided that he would bring Josh for a visit
to SeaWorld. Josh's eyes became as big as saucers when
he encountered, up close, the huge black-and-white forms
of the whales during their performance. After enjoying the
show, Matt and Josh joined Amy backstage. Most of the
staff had met Amy's husband and child before, and they
made a fuss over how much Josh had grown.

Amy asked Kim Lee if Matt and Josh could watch as
she and her coach worked with Taat and her baby, Kagan,
who was being trained toward weaning. When Amy fed
Taat, the mother whale took some of the fish and gave it
to her youngster. Kagan pushed the fish around, tasting
it and spitting it out. Each time Josh saw the baby whale
spit its food, he laughed and pointed.

"It looks like Kagan's just playing with his food," Matt said.

"That's right," Kim Lee said. "Baby whales start getting their teeth at around three months of age, which is the exact time that the mother whales start to offer the babies small fish. It will be a while before he's fully weaned. At this point Taat gives him fish to play with. We also help her along, giving the baby fish to help him get used to them. As he gets older, he'll start chewing on them and eventually will start swallowing them. Soon after that, he'll be off his mama's milk and eating on his own."

"He really hangs close to his mom all the time, doesn't he?" Matt said.

"You bet," Amy agreed. "As he's being weaned off of Mom's milk, he'll start to wander and investigate on his own. When he's weaned and gets more confident about the environment, he'll start swimming away from his mother. When that happens, we'll try to get the baby to pay more attention to us by offering small fish, toys, or ourselves at the sides of the pools for him to look at. When he starts to come over, we'll give him tactile—that's slang for rubdowns. Tactile is a baby whale's favorite. Everything we do will be designed to help him feel more and more secure in his environment. But just like humans, a baby whale's mom will keep a close eye on him to make sure that he doesn't wander too far. Our relationships with the whales have to be strong so that moms trust us with their babies."

After observing for a while, Matt said, "I've got to get Josh home, but this was great. I learned a lot. In fact, I want to start using some of what I saw today in getting this guy to be less dependent on his pacifier during the day."

"That's good, Matt," Kim Lee said. "I'm a mom, and like Amy, I've learned so much about parenting here at work. The A-B-C principles of behavior are the same for animals and people. It's good to always keep in mind what's behind these 'pacifier' behaviors. Whether it's an animal or a child, they usually hang onto them because of insecurity. In weaning them away, we need to be patient, substituting other things that fulfill these needs until they're ready to give them up."

"Sounds good," Matt said. "Thanks, Kim Lee."

That evening Amy had a late meeting and didn't get home until Josh was asleep. Matt was eager to tell her how he'd started on the new strategy. "You know how Josh hangs onto his pacifier all the time?" he said. "I learned today at SeaWorld that a child needs something that gives comfort when he's a little insecure. So I let Josh keep the pacifier when we were driving, and also when we stopped at the hardware store on the way home. In those environments I figured it was okay for now.

"When we got home, I went and got his blanket, figuring that's a good substitute for the comfort because he likes the feel of it. When he took it, I held out my hand for the pacifier and he gave it to me. I really praised him, and he gave me a big smile. Then later when I was getting him ready for bed, he was cooperating and not fussing, so I gave him the pacifier. He settled right down and was asleep in minutes."

"Honey, I am so proud of you," said Amy. "What you did shows that you're not just focusing on the behavior but 'thinking behind it' to the need that motivates it. As long as we do that, we're pointing ourselves toward what works. I see it in my work all the time. Maybe I'm impatient with something that doesn't seem to go right with the animals. But then I think, *What's behind this?* There's always an answer, and that leads me to the solution. So, good job, honey."

"I've got to say I learned it from your coach, Kim Lee."

Amy nodded. "Kim Lee is amazing. She's got two kids of her own and a master's in child development. I'm so lucky to be working with her. She's my coach in more ways than one."

That Sunday afternoon the Sheldrakes were invited to a barbecue at the home of Bob and Maria Castone, a couple they hadn't seen for months. They were looking forward to seeing the Castones' boy, Eric, who was a few months older than Josh.

"I wonder if Eric is as demanding as he was when he was smaller," Amy said.

"They've sure had their hands full with him," Matt agreed.

The visit and cookout went along smoothly until a teenage neighbor who had been hired to watch the two little boys took them inside to the playroom. After visiting a while outside, the parents went indoors to check on the kids. When they opened the playroom door, they saw piles of toys scattered about the room. In the middle of them sat Eric. The moment he saw his parents, he screamed for attention. It took them a while to calm him down. Josh looked confused at his friend's upset, and Amy and Matt chose to ignore it. Later when they were driving home, they talked about it.

"Man," said Matt, "they've really heaped the toys on Eric, haven't they?"

Amy shrugged. "No more than your folks gave our son his last birthday," she said. "If you'll remember, though, we put most of them away. I've been holding them back. That way Josh doesn't get bored with them. He plays with a few; then I hide one of them and bring out another. Later when I bring out the toy he'd played with before, it's like it's all new for him again."

Matt chuckled. "Learn that from the whales, did ya?"

"What do *you* think?" Amy said with a smile.

BUILDING HEALTHY ATTITUDES TOWARD POSSESSIONS

Set things up for success

There are times, like holidays and birthdays, when toys and gifts accumulate in a child's life. You can use these times to teach a healthy nondependency on things. Don't surround your child with toys. Instead, arrange them in baskets, have one basket out at a time, and rotate baskets occasionally. Keep introducing the same toys; if a cherished object is put away for a time, bringing it out creates a delightful remembering and freshness of outlook.

Ignore failure and/or redirect

Suppose your child asks for a toy that has been put away for a while. You can direct attention toward an object or experience that is already in the environment. If you lose or break a possession, try to model a good attitude ("I appreciated it while I had it!") so that your child can begin to develop an attitude of nonattachment. If a toy of hers is broken or lost, help her to say, "I had fun with that." The same can be said of enjoyable but temporary experiences such as trips and special entertainment events.

58

Give a Whale Done!

Acknowledge with praise and affection each and every step that indicates your child is able to exercise care and cleanliness of possessions. Guide your child toward cleaning and maintaining her toys, as well as putting them away carefully, and give hugs, stars, and other Whale Dones as rewards. As your child demonstrates freedom from attachment, praise and acknowledge this attitude. A reward might be a special card or meal, rather than another material object like a toy.

CHAPTER

Seven

Not Just Yours
Teaching Your Child to Share

"**T**ODAY IS ABOUT teaching the whales to share," Clint announced. He'd had the trainers move a pair of killer whales into one pool for practice. Addressing the three trainees, he said, "Whales are like kids, in a way. They have to learn to share their toys and food and other things." Clint gestured toward the whales, which were busy playing with the toys the trainers had tossed to them. "Also like young children, their goals are to get attention and acquire resources. So we have to teach them to share."

The "toys" were truly whale-size. One was a fifty-five-gallon barrel. Another was a six-foot-diameter plastic ball. "We can't even lift that," Clint said, "but the whales toss it around like it was nothing, even flipping it out of the water. Now, let's see what Jody does to begin teaching

Tutan to share with Taat." Amy was taking notes as she watched the experienced trainer playing catch with Tutan. Jody would toss the toy—a thick tie-down rope—to Tutan, and the whale would swim it back to her, pushing it with its nose. "Bear in mind that what Jody is using is Tutan's favorite toy," Clint said. "The next stage is to get the whales to share with each other."

As Amy and the others watched, Jody gave Tutan's toy to Taat, who immediately began to play with it. When Tutan made as if to turn and swim toward Taat to get his toy back, Jody gave the "stay with me" hand signal. She then presented him with a new, very large flotation toy he had never seen before. He swam off and began frolicking with it. After a while she called both whales to her and switched toys between them. Now Tutan had his old favorite back, and Taat had the new toy. The object was evident: get both whales accustomed to having their toys exchanged, and prevent attachment and trouble.

Later at lunch, Amy was sitting next to Clint. "I liked what we learned today about sharing," she said.

Clint replied, "Well, it's not always that easy. We have to practice sharing with the whales a lot, especially with new items."

"I find myself applying a lot of what we learn here to my two-year-old at home. Do you have any advice for a parent like me who's facing this sharing issue?"

Clint nodded. "Tiny kids don't usually talk to communicate their desire for what they want, but they can make noise, so they do a lot of that. I think the most important thing is to be proactive—to think ahead and develop the thing you want your child to learn. First of all, you must understand what these drives—getting attention and securing resources—are all about. Then you have to train your child how to get what he wants in the right way.

"Most parents want to teach their kids to share," Clint went on, "but they unknowingly wait for trouble to develop, and then the child's only 'training' is through a confrontation with another child, which leaves a residue of hurt or fear or protectiveness. The principle is the same one you know, the one we use again and again with the animals: *Build from the very beginning toward winning. Set things up to get the behavior you want from your child, and don't wait for the behavior you* don't *want to be his first experience.*

"Remember how Tutan was helped to experience giving up his toy by having his attention redirected to a new plaything? That can work the same way with kids. You might wait until your boy is playing with his favorite toy and then say, 'Could I see that?' or otherwise show that you want it. Then when your child offers it to you, make a big deal of it—'Oh, that's so *good*—you shared your toy with Mommy!'"

When lunch was over, Clint said, "Let's go see how this principle plays out at mealtime."

The group moved to another tank where Kusti, the biggest killer whale in the group, was swimming with some others. As Amy and her fellow trainees Steve and

Lorraine set up the feeding buckets, Amy noted that while the other whales immediately swam over to eat, Kusti stayed at the far end.

"How is it that the dominant killer whale is choosing to eat last?" she asked in wonder.

"We trained him that way," said Clint. "Otherwise, the other whales would always be shoved out of the way. Why have trouble at mealtime?" Clint got a crafty look on his face. "So, maybe you've been around here long enough to tell us what we did to get this result?"

The three trainees looked at each other and smiled. "Guess this is a pop quiz," said Steve. "Okay, I'll start. You probably worked with Kusti and one other whale, giving them food at the same time. Then after a while, you looked for a time when the big guy waited a short time and immediately rewarded him."

Clint nodded.

Amy took a turn. "Finally, you added more whales at feeding time, rewarding Kusti every time he waited, until he was getting special stuff for going last."

"That's right," Clint said, looking pleased. "The whale learned that if he waited, he won. There's almost nothing you can't train animals to do, *if* you always remain positive, ignore mistakes, and be there to celebrate what they do right. Speaking of which, that was a great analysis you three did just now. Pizza's on me!"

That weekend Sharon, Amy's sister, phoned to say she would be in town and would like to come by with her daughter Pattie for a short visit. Seeing this as an opportunity to train Josh in sharing, Amy told Sharon what she was planning and asked her to bring along one of Pattie's favorite toys.

The next afternoon the mothers took the children to a nearby park. Amy had Josh bring along his Mikie, a beloved stuffed bear. For a while the mothers sat and watched the two youngsters playing in a sandbox. Then Amy said, "Let's see what happens when we give them their toys." Things went well, Josh pushing his Mikie along a road he had built in the sand while Pattie rocked her stuffed kitty dressed as a girl.

Amy went over and said, "Josh, could I see your Mikie for a minute?" Josh gave her the toy, and Amy said, "Thank you, Joshie, that was great! You shared with Mommy so nicely!" She handed back the Mikie, and signaled to her sister to repeat the transaction with Pattie. The mothers did several such exchanges, praising their tots repeatedly for sharing.

"Now comes the moment," Amy said, giving Sharon a wink. Turning to Josh, she asked him for the Mikie a third time. Receiving it, she praised Josh. Then she said, "Josh, could Mommy let Pattie see your Mikie?" Josh looked at Pattie. He looked at the Mikie. Then he came over and took his toy from Amy. Amy was disappointed. Her chagrin turned to joy, however, when Josh handed his

Mikie to Pattie. "Oh, Josh!" Amy exclaimed. "Momma's so proud of you!" Sharon applauded as well.

Now it was Sharon's turn. Having had Pattie practice giving her doll away, she now repeated Amy's plea. And little Pattie, with a sweet smile, handed her kitty to Josh. Both mothers again were profuse in their celebration. "Yay, Pattie! Pattie shared!" they chanted.

THE FUN OF SHARING

Set things up for success

Play is work for two- and three-year-olds, and it involves important learning. A playing child this age is on a kind of mission, so being asked to share a toy may be a rude interruption. If your child understands, you can go over the guidelines ahead of time: "Today I'd like to see if you can share your toys." As you are adding gifts and toys to your child's life, be aware of opportunities for sharing. As in the story, look for and set up opportunities to reward any behavior that approximates the one you want. A parent's own generosity is the first ongoing line of training about sharing. Your child needs opportunities to watch you share and show delight in doing so. Use the practice demonstrated in the story, rewarding and verbally praising your child each time she gives up something willingly.

Ignore failure and/or redirect

If your child refuses to share, you might demonstrate by giving some other item to the other child, showing great delight in doing so. Early on, establish this by playing with your child's toys yourself. Gradually introduce chances for your child to share with other family members with whom she feels comfortable. If two children want the same toy, say, "Here's a block for you, and one for you, and one for me. Now, I give my block to you. Will you give it back?"

Give a Whale Done!

Willingness to share represents a big step in your child's development. Any action that looks like sharing—handing a toy to another, offering a bite of food—should be praised with delight as a step forward. You are helping build lifelong values of friendship, generosity and nonattachment. Begin to build your child's habit of sharing by calling immediate attention to each behavior in that direction. Be alert to reward *approximate* successes, for progress in this area tends to occur in small steps.

CHAPTER

Eight

An Overused Word and a Visit to the Dentist

"NO!"

When she saw Josh putting a pencil in his mouth, Amy yelled and ran to take it away from him. A few minutes later the boy picked up a small antique vase, whereupon Amy again yelled, "No!" Josh started to sob; soon he was wailing at the top of his lungs. Amy knew that she had scared him this time, but the vase was a valuable gift from her grandmother. Feeling sorry, she went over to Josh and gently took the vase away from him. After placing it on a high shelf, she turned to Josh and hugged him until he stopped sobbing.

As often happened, an occurrence at her workplace opened the young mother's eyes.

The next day, Clint was telling the group about his early work with killer whales. "Back then we, mere humans, were trying to tell an eight- to ten-thousand-pound killer whale what to do. Think how silly that is! I mean, there we were, dealing with the top predator in the ocean, and we were trying to tell them no! How nutty is that?"

"Trying to make an animal do something is not that different from trying to make a human being do something. It doesn't go over well. What is so much more palatable is to *ask* them to do it—and then *reward* them for doing it! What is the goal of any kind of leadership or influencing? It's to have the animal, or person, *want* to do what you want done, on their own. Back then we had the beginnings of an understanding of that notion, but we didn't act it out. Our mistakes had really serious consequences. Because of the size and capabilities of these animals, we did get hurt sometimes.

"For instance, when we thought about getting in the water with them, we realized right away that these whales could be dangerous. You've seen how rough they get when they play with each other. Imagine having one of them bump you in the water the way they bump each other! We had to teach them not to treat us like we were one of them—that compared to animals of their size, we human beings are fragile. At first they so enjoyed having us in the water with them that they didn't want us to get out!

"We didn't know much about the A-B-C principle back then. We were almost primitive in our approaches.

We were okay with rewarding the behaviors we wanted, but we hadn't yet learned to ignore the wrong ones. So we thought we had to teach them what *not* to do."

Clint's listeners laughed, enjoying this. Obviously they were on the side of the whale. Clint, too, was emphasizing the absurdity in the story. "We were difficult learners, but the whales finally taught us. We started paying attention to and rewarding only the behaviors we wanted, and ignoring or redirecting the rest. We used only food as a reinforcer then, but over the years we've developed very close bonds with these animals by paying attention to what each whale wants and likes."

That afternoon Amy confided in her coach, Kim Lee. "I feel so bad yelling *no* at Josh all the time. He wants to pick up everything, it seems, and it's getting worse. There has to be a better way of handling this."

Kim Lee smiled. "Have you noticed that the word *no* is something these animals never hear around here?" she said.

Amy thought about it.

"That word is usually the first word kids hear from their moms and dads when they're exploring their worlds," Kim Lee went on. "Using it too much can lead to trouble."

"You're right," Amy agreed. "It's like that's all I say to Josh lately, and now he's even saying it back to me when I ask him something. I'm using that *no* word far too often now that Josh has started exploring the house, touching and picking up everything. Most of the time as soon as he finds something new, it automatically goes into his mouth."

Kim Lee nodded. "Kids are like whales when they're young," she said. "They're inquisitive and like to explore their new world, and the mouth is an exploratory tool. This is an area where the first rule—the one about setting up for success—is key."

Amy thought about that. "In other words," she reflected, "it makes sense to arrange the environment to be free of things you don't want them to touch or to go into their mouths."

"Right. My husband and I went through the same thing with our son. Saying *no* a lot seems to kind of hang a cloud over things whenever the child hears it. It's often said loudly, too, so it sounds unpleasant. The more times it's said, the more the kid's liable to start feeling, *I never do anything right.* Also, it's calling a lot of attention to the behavior you *don't* want."

Amy thought about this. "By putting emphasis on what an animal or child does wrong," she said, "you're keeping it in his mind and can actually end up training him to repeat it."

"Right again," Kim Lee said. "You can't totally get rid of the word *no* with children, but you can drastically reduce your use of it. Also, when we started rewarding our boy for *not* touching things, we found ourselves saying *no* less often. If you can cut down your random use of the word, then those times when you *do* have to use it—like when Josh is running out into the street or is about to touch something hot—it will mean something. There's nothing really wrong with the word *no*, but saying it loudly and sharply should be reserved for times of clear and present danger."

That evening Amy told Matt about her discussion with Kim Lee. The two parents went around the house, picking up any and all objects they didn't want Josh handling; they found there were quite a few of them. Next they explored for any sharp edges or surfaces that could injure the youngster.

"That about completes the stripping of the environment," Matt said, smiling. "This is going to make everything a lot easier. As Josh gets older and understands more, we can start to move all these untouchable objects back in place."

"And think of all the times we just saved ourselves from shouting *no*," Amy said.

The next day Amy was asked to take part in a whale's oral examination. The patient was Kusti, an animal Amy had been working with to develop a trusting relationship. Kim Lee and Amy went to the pool where Kusti was swimming, and the coach pressed a button labeled "Callback Tone." It rang an underwater tone that signaled "Stop what you are doing and return to me, and you'll be rewarded." Kusti immediately swam over, and Amy gave the whale some fish. Then she gave Kusti the hand signal Kim Lee had shown her for opening the mouth. Kusti's cavernous mouth yawned open, revealing impressive rows of big teeth. Somewhat gingerly, Amy did as Kim Lee had demonstrated previously, massaging Kusti's gums and using a Waterpik to clean around the teeth.

"This is amazing," Amy said. "She doesn't mind at all."

"That's because of the work we've done to desensitize her," said Kim Lee. "After teaching Kusti to hold her mouth open like this, we gradually began touching all the parts of her mouth to get her used to the feeling of our poking around in there. This way, when we do have to drill her teeth, she'll be accustomed to us fussing with her mouth, and it won't be a big problem."

"Did the desensitizing process take a long time?" Amy asked as she worked toward the rear teeth.

"It sure wasn't an all-at-once operation for a new whale," Kim Lee said. She added, "Of course, you already know what preceded the actual work on the teeth." Amy was silent. When Kim Lee added, "Right?" she realized she was being quizzed.

"Uh, sure," Amy said, thinking fast. "You did a lot of lead-up to make the whole thing a lot of fun for Kusti. You always brought her here so she associated the area with good times. Then when you trained her to open her mouth, you got her used to the brush, and so on."

Kim Lee was silent.

"How'd I do?" Amy said. "Did I leave anything out?"

"Just all the intermittent praising for each bit of progress Kusti made. But I figured that was understood, since you see us doing it here all the time. Yeah, you get a Whale Done."

Driving home that evening, Amy was thinking of the upcoming visit she was to make to the dentist with Josh. When she reached home, she phoned the office and left a message to have the dentist call her on her cell phone the next day at her lunch hour.

"Hi, Dr. Renning," Amy said after opening her phone and checking the caller ID. "Thanks for calling me back."

"Hello, Amy," the dentist's friendly voice came back. "Everything all right?"

"Yes, everything's fine. Reason I called is, I'll be bringing my two-year-old Josh in for his first visit later this month. I wondered if you and I can work out a plan for a sort of preliminary visit in the next few days."

"You mean to get him used to the office and to me?" the dentist asked.

"Exactly. I wondered whether you could even take some of the stuffed toys and other fun things you keep out in the waiting room and have them around in the examination room."

The dentist welcomed her plan. "I've got to tell you, Amy," he said, "I wish more parents would think of this kind of thing. A child's first visit is so important, but despite my best efforts to be friendly, it rarely goes well."

The more they talked, the more enthusiastic Dr. Renning became. "How about music?" he said. "Do you have a favorite song of Josh's on a CD that we could play? And does he have some special thing he likes that we could make a sort of theme for the room?"

By the time the call ended, the collaborators had decided to have Josh come dressed in his superhero suit, and Amy would bring along the rousing song they always played when he wore it. Josh would likely climb into the chair when he saw his Mikie there with a bib on, as if he'd just been examined. All the instruments would be on display, but none would be used. It would just be a get-acquainted visit, with the emphasis on fun.

When the preliminary visit took place, it came off without a hitch. After confirming their appointment for Josh's exam in two weeks, Amy and Dr. Renning winked at each other.

"Did you like Dr. Renning?" Amy asked Josh on the way home.

"Yes!" said Josh with enthusiasm.

Amy smiled and gave herself a mental pat on the back.

AVOIDING THE OVERUSE OF *NO*

Set things up for success

Reducing the frequency of scolding, reprimanding, or even using the word *no*, is worth the effort. It keeps you from adopting the unfortunate "bad cop" role toward your child. Sometimes you can use your child's name just to get his attention as a redirection before using *no*. Systematically removing items you don't wish your child to touch is one way to avoid overusing the word. Introducing your child to new environments in a way that emphasizes fun and enjoyment, as Amy did with Josh at the dentist, is another way to ensure successful orientation. This capitalizes on the issue of *core memory*—the tendency to associate a person, object, or environment with first impressions of it.

Ignore failure and/or redirect

If your child picks up or plays with something you don't want him to have, call a toy or other distracting element to his attention. Always be careful not to reward the behavior that you *don't* want. In potentially uncertain situations such as doctor and dentist visits, children look to their parents to see how to respond. If you remain calm and relaxed, treating the situation as fun, your child will follow suit.

Give a Whale Done!

Give a Whale Done whenever you see your child following directions in not touching items you have identified as off-limits. A reward might be a Whale Done sticker, crayons, or other small item. Immediacy of reward is key to shaping behavior with the whales; act accordingly by making sure you have these Whale Done items with you or handy at all times, so you can reward on the spot. Make an enjoyable "test" visit with your child to the doctor or dentist. When your child negotiates a "real" visit successfully, a celebration is in order.

CHAPTER

Nine

Word Gets Around
Whale Done Parenting of All Ages

AS IN MANY modern communities, people in the Sheldrakes' neighborhood hardly knew each other. Almost without exception the parents worked; absent all day from home, they spent evenings and weekends with their families. Although Amy and Matt were on a first-name basis with their immediate neighbors, they would not have known the others except for a plan that had been instituted by people on their street before they moved in. This was the block party.

Every few months a notice would come around, stating the date, time, and address at which the next neighborhood potluck was to be held. These were always enjoyable gatherings, and Matt and Amy were happy to participate and get to know people in their area. Little did they dream that the upcoming block party was to be the means by which they could help others learn the Whale Done method of parenting.

Walking to the nearby party site with Josh, they observed a crowd filling a driveway, where tables were laden with food and people were eating and talking excitedly. The two had hardly placed their casserole on a table when they were approached by a couple slightly older than themselves.

"Hi," the husband said. "I'm Ted Wilkins, and this is Marge." Pointing to a large house across the street, he said, "We live over there. And you are Amy and Matt Sheldrake, right?"

"Right," said Matt.

"I'm a superhero!" interjected Josh, staring up at the newcomers.

Marge smiled. "We have a couple of superheroes, too," she said with a chuckle. She turned to Amy. "Matter of fact, that's what we'd like to talk to you about. You work at SeaWorld?"

Amy smiled and nodded.

"That must be fascinating. Well—" Marge hesitated, looking at her husband "—we heard from our friends who live next door to you—you know, Donna and Jim Giacomo? Anyway, they told us you're using some of the techniques of animal training in your raising of Josh here."

Amy and Matt looked at each other. "Uh, that's right, but we—"

"Oh, don't get the wrong idea," Ted Wilkins put in. "We think it's great."

Just then Ted and Marge were each jostled and grabbed by a noisy, grinning boy. One had been chasing the other, and they were using their parents as bases. As the Wilkins tried to calm the rambunctious, red-faced children, the clamor continued. The boys tried to grab at each other and hide behind the adults. Finally, Ted said angrily, "That's *enough*, now! You guys just quiet down! I want you to meet some neighbors of ours—"

But the boys were off again, screaming and darting in and out between adults who tried not to spill their paper plates of food as they were bumped.

Marge's face reddened. "Those are our boys—Steven, ten, and Gabriel, nine. They're the reason we wanted to know more about your whale training methods."

While she spoke, her husband gestured to several others to join them. When they came over, Ted announced, "Folks, these are Amy and Matt Sheldrake. Amy works at SeaWorld." As Amy and Matt made acquaintances, Ted added, "Marge and I were just asking Amy whether the ways they use to train the killer whales can be used to train children."

There was a pause. Then a man in the back snickered and said, "Yeah, right. What are you gonna do with your kid, throw 'em a fish?" Several in the crowd chuckled at the remark.

Taking no offense, Amy laughed and said mildly, "No, we don't do that. But applying the methods in working with our two-year-old has produced some good results."

As the audience showed more interest, Matt spoke up. "As I learned from Amy, it's really a matter of what you pay attention to. Tell them about getting Josh to pick up his toys, honey."

Amy recounted how she ignored Josh's making a mess but celebrated when he did pick things up. Heads began nodding and more couples drifted over to listen.

A woman said, "My name's Letitia, and I'm a single mom. I'm having a hard time with my boy Alex using profanity." She pointed to a gangly teen standing at a serving table and consuming food. "Do you think this method would work on a teenager? And if so, how would you go about it?"

"First of all, Letitia," Amy said, "do you use that kind of language yourself?"

Letitia, momentarily taken aback, replied, "Well, I suppose all of us cuss on occasion."

"That's where you can start to do what we call setting the child up for success. You eliminate any reinforcement for doing the undesirable behavior. So you can start with cutting down on your own use of profanity. And whenever you slip and use a bad word, you can apologize to Alex."

Letitia said thoughtfully, "Yes, I can do that."

"The other thing I would recommend is to choose a good time to calmly sit down with your boy and discuss the matter. Maybe you set things up by fixing his favorite meal for dinner, and then say, 'I need your help on something. As you know, this swearing business is not okay with me. I even do it myself sometimes, and I want you to call my attention to it whenever you hear me do it. Another thing I promise to do is stop yelling at you when I hear you cuss. But I'd like to know you're working on it as well.' This is to let Alex know in a kind way that his behavior bothers you. After that, you need to go to work on the really powerful part of the method."

"What's that?" Letitia asked.

Amy said, "Changing what you pay attention to. It means making a big deal when he *doesn't* swear—like, just casually mentioning, 'You've really been paying attention to the no-cussing rule, and I am proud of your effort.' If he violates the rule, sit down with him and revisit the guidelines, emphasizing that swearing is not acceptable, but that you stand ready to reward his avoiding it. And follow through on this, recognizing every effort on his part. If he starts to cuss in your presence, then stops and corrects himself, praise him. This shifting of attention from what your child does wrong to what he does right is the real magic of what we call the Whale Done way."

There was silence for a moment as Amy's listeners ruminated over her advice. Finally, the man who had laughed spoke up. "My name's Jim, and I gotta say that *not* paying attention to the bad behavior and paying *lots* of attention to the good sounds so radical it might even work."

"Nothing else has been working with getting my daughter to do her homework," said his wife. "I think we'll give it a try."

"Good," said Amy. "You really need to explain to your child why homework is important, then set things up so she'll be successful. Agree on a homework time—preferably right after coming in from school and before TV or other distractions—and stick to it. Have her report each day to you after she completes the homework."

Jim spoke up. "I guess we'd look for an instance to catch Jess when she has done her homework, and praise her. Is that right?"

"Right," Amy replied. "Every chance you can, celebrate her sticking to the rules. Also, you may need to look at your issue of the homework as really just a worry on your part. I mean, does Jess's homework get done at all? Seems like you'd hear from her teachers if it didn't. Just your staying off her case about the homework—I hate to use the word *nagging*, but we all tend to do it—probably represents a real change and wouldn't fail to be registered with your daughter. Then some night at dinner one of you says to the other, 'Jess has been getting her homework done on her own,' and the other one tells Jess, 'Wow! I'm really proud of you!' That would reinforce the trend."

Someone else asked, "Can you tell us some more about the animal training techniques?"

"Sure," said Amy, feeling more at ease with her audience. "There's something we call the A-B-C principle. *A* stands for *activator*; that's whatever prompts B, the *behav-*

ior. C stands for *consequence*, which is what follows as a result of the behavior. Of the three elements, we say that C is the most important. Now, let's see how this works with a behavior one of you is trying to get your child to stop. I know you'll all probably have to search for an example." The group laughed.

"I've got one," said a man Amy recognized as her neighbor from across the street, Joe Travers. "My son is always teasing his sister. It drives me crazy."

"Okay, teasing is the behavior. What would be a likely activator, or trigger, for that behavior?"

"It could be anything his sister does. For instance, she likes to watch what he calls 'baby shows' on TV."

"Okay," said Amy. "A is something sister does. B is brother's teasing. What's the C that follows?"

"That's easy," said Joe. "I yell at him to stop. I tell him he's going to lose his allowance or can't watch television."

"So, yells and threats. Has that worked?"

"Not so far," Joe said.

Amy nodded. "So, if you were to change the consequence, what would it be?"

"Like you said: ignore the teasing. That might require my wearing ear plugs!"

"Ignore it if it's minor. On the other hand, if it's hateful or destructive, as a parent you must act on it. So first communicate that it's inappropriate to tease. You might *redirect* it. Sit down calmly with your boy and appeal to the best in him. Say, 'Hey, how about saying something *nice* to your sister? If you were to treat her better, I bet

she'd do something nice for you. What do you think?'
Then when the boy agrees, you encourage him: 'Now
you're talking!'"

Joe nodded.

"Now," Amy said, "besides responding by ignoring or
redirecting the teasing, what else is called for?"

"Starting to really pay attention to when he's nice to
his sister. You know, now that I think of it, he really likes
her. Sometimes I see him being really good to her."

"So, what will you do now when you notice that
good behavior?"

"Notice the heck out of it, I guess."

"Exactly. I think you can also work with your daughter. A definite consequence of his teasing is seeing her get
upset. So let her in on the game by teaching her to ignore
his teasing. Eliminating that payoff may be a big part of
the solution."

The pause that followed suggested that the others
were further considering this new philosophy.

"I don't want to take up the whole party with this discussion," Amy said. "But this step of rewarding success
might require parents to do some research on their children. I don't often compare human beings to animals. We
don't always act like animals, but when it comes to the
science of changing behavior, we *are* alike —we respond
to attention. So, what are some ways we could reward and
recognize Joe's son when he's nice to his sister?"

"Wait a minute," Letitia broke in. "Are you saying
that this kid is going to stop teasing right away, just

because you stop paying attention to him when he does it?"

Ted, the host, piped up at this point. "Maybe he won't stop right away," he said, "But if there's enough reward and recognition for doing the opposite, pretty soon the boy is going to get the picture. He'll say to himself, *Hmm, this is interesting. There's a connection. When I tease my sister, my dad and my sister ignore me. But when I'm nice to her, I get the heck praised out of me.* This kid is no dummy. He's eventually going to go with what he gets attention for."

The nods and smiles around the group showed that Ted's comment had struck home.

"Thanks, Ted," said Amy. "I admit that when you first hear about this approach, it may be shocking because it's such a reversal from what we normally do. But when I first saw it working at the park, I began to see that I had been unwittingly contributing to some of the behavior problems I was having with Josh. When Matt and I stopped reacting to what he did wrong and rewarded what he did right, things began to change."

"The more I think about it, the more it makes sense," said Letitia.

Amy smiled. "My boss is fond of saying that the way to get people to do what you want is to *catch them doing things right.* If that's the only thing you remember from all this, I'll be glad."

"Can you share a couple more key points with us?" asked Ted, acting as moderator.

"If you're interested," Amy said. The others nodded.

"One thing would be to set your child up for success. At the park, rather than being hit-or-miss about it or waiting around for the whales to do something we like, we concentrate on arranging things for them to be successful. The way we do this is to observe them very closely; to find out what their habits are, their internal clocks and timelines, their likes and dislikes. What one animal seeks in the way of a reward for a good job might not appeal to another animal at all. They are individuals with different histories, likes and dislikes, just as we are.

"Likewise, we have to study our children. When is each one most likely to behave favorably? How can we set up an environment in which that is likely to happen, so we can catch them at it and reward them with a praising or a hug? What means most to them that we could provide as rewards or incentives? So often it's the setting up for success that is the key, so it needs to be thought out carefully."

"So a particular food or toy or fun activity might be a reward?" asked Marge.

"Absolutely," said Amy, adding, "Remember, folks, this is not easy. We parents have a tendency to go negative and try to stop bad behavior in its tracks. It's much harder, and takes more effort and time, to stay on the positive track. But the results are better and much more lasting. They are results that help our relationships with our kids, instead of doing harm to them."

"I'm a single dad, and this sure has been enlightening for me," said a man at the edge of the group. "I can see that the biggest challenge is going to be changing myself. I have to stop rewarding behavior in my kids I don't like—in fact, I have to start ignoring it. That's going to be tough. But I sure am going to start looking for ways to catch my kids doing things right."

To this there was agreement all around. The people thanked Amy and gradually drifted away, talking about what they had heard.

As they were walking home, Matt told Amy, "You did a nice job, honey."

She smiled and said, "I heard somewhere that the best way to learn something is to teach it. It just might be true."

WHALE DONE WITH ALL AGES

Set things up for success

Although this book focuses mostly on using the Whale Done approach in the raising of children up to five years old, we emphatically state that, with modifications depending on age and experience, these methods, based on behavioral science, can be used successfully with virtually anyone. That is because all people are in a constant search for happiness and "what's in it for me?" Being praised and recognized for what they do right feeds directly into that motive. Help your child associate the agreements you make regarding her behavior with fun, relaxation, and enjoyment. Introduce an air of lightness or adventure by making a game of the change. Thinking things out carefully and planning ahead usually pave the way to a successful conclusion.

Ignore failure and/or redirect

With young children, use redirection when appropriate. With older children and adults, use reasoning. In parenting older children, verbal communication can play a much larger part. Include your true feelings about the issue (disappointment, for example) as well as a nonblaming description of your child's behavior and the impact of that behavior on you, the household, or others. (Example: "When you bring home low grades like this, I feel sad because it is so far below what I'm pretty sure you can accomplish.") Be willing to look at and reevaluate your approach when you are not getting the desirable behavior. Whenever you can, steer attention toward something for which you can reward your child.

Give a Whale Done!

Be sure to include rewards that you know from experience will be appealing to your child. For instance, one sibling might respond best to verbal recognition. Another might rise to special family times. For a third, a new tool set for his hobby might ring the bell.

Ten

Puppy Love
Teaching Pet Care

I T WAS A RAINY morning and the SeaWorld coaches and trainees were gathered in the training room. Head trainer Clint said, "I noticed some of you were working on the animals' dental hygiene the other day. It made me think about what a far cry those procedures are from what we went through back when I first started in this job."

"Who was president then, Clint?" Jared, a trainer coach, asked from the back of the room. "George Washington?" Good-natured kidding was part of the SeaWorld culture, and the remark brought guffaws from the audience.

"I can't remember," Clint replied, playing along. "I just know it was back in the horse-and-buggy days. Anyway, looking back to those times, I can't believe how naive we were, how lacking in even a rudimentary understanding of these killer whales, compared to today. We were going strictly by trial and error.

"As you know, when we're working with a baby whale, we spend a lot of time before getting in the water with him, establishing trust with him and the mother. Getting the mom's trust is the main thing. She has to trust us tremendously to allow us in the water with her little baby."

Clint paused and smiled. "I remember back in 1985 when the first baby whale was born here. I went in the water to get some underwater video coverage of the birth. So there I am, next to this mother whale, when she starts to go into labor. I'm shooting away, realizing that she's in a lot of pain but figuring I could depend on the relationship I'd built with her. But the mom isn't thinking about our relationship at all; in fact, she's finding me a serious distraction. Finally, she swims up close to me and snaps her jaws at me—not biting me but telling me she was upset with me. Believe me, I got out of there! No telling what would have happened to me if I'd stayed around."

The listeners seemed to heave a group sigh.

"So now," Clint continued, "after years of building trust with a female killer whale before she gets pregnant, we know that when the baby is born, she'll be extremely protective at first. We have to show her all over again that we mean her and her baby no harm. Killer whales are very tactile, so the rubdown is the main reinforcer we use with the mom and the baby.

"When the baby is about two weeks old, we touch the mom and then start testing whether she'll let us touch the baby. As she allows us to get closer, we start by putting our arms in the water to rub the baby. Next we move into shallow water, and rub both mom and baby. After a while, the calf starts to swim around us and investigate us. We keep watching the mom to make sure it's okay with her. When the baby pushes us—a killer whale's standard way of getting acquainted with a peer—we go limp in the water so there's no response to that. If the baby opens its mouth to grab an arm or wetsuit, we pull the arm slowly away and use our hands to gently close the baby's mouth, then reinforce it with a rubdown.

"It's through a series of small interactions like that that we teach the baby whale what we want it to do," Clint concluded. "As with most everything we do here, it takes time, but it pays off."

Clint's stories served Amy well the following week when she and Matt visited an animal rescue shelter to pick out a puppy. Amy had planned this adoption for a long time. For her, it was more than a matter of having a family pet. She had grown up with animals, and she wanted to instill in her son the same love and understanding of all creatures. Besides the usual fun of having a pet, she and Matt wanted to use the puppy to teach Josh to be gentle and caring not only with animals but with kids and adults and all creatures. At the shelter the family spent much time looking at puppies. Finally, they decided on a Labrador pup. As Matt drove home, Amy sat beside him holding the puppy, with Josh strapped in the back seat.

Amy said, "I've learned that most dog bites occur with very young children. Without training and example, when kids see a dog, they follow their natural inclination to reach out and explore. They see the floppy ears and the wagging tail as something to grab, and they like to take a handful of fur and twist it. The dog, of course, doesn't go for any of that. In fact, one single interaction like that might teach a young dog to think 'hurt' when it sees a small human. So we need to train both Josh and what's-his-name here—by the way, what about a name for him?"

"About that," said Matt with a wry smile. "This little guy looks to me like an Oscar."

"Oscar!" Amy cried in horror. "You gotta be kidding me!"

"Oshka!" Josh shouted. When Amy turned and looked back at him she saw that Josh was pointing to the dog with a big smile. "Oshka! Oshka!" he repeated, obviously pleased with the name for his new acquaintance.

Matt and Amy looked at each other. "Oshka?" they both said together.

"It could be, like, a Native American word," Matt said hopefully.

"At least it's better than *Oscar*," Amy replied.

Josh's excitement over the new puppy knew no bounds. When they reached home, Matt and Amy found it difficult to get his attention for a story, but Matt managed to settle down with Josh and a favorite book on the couch. Meanwhile, Amy went to the kitchen with the pup to prepare things for Josh's orientation to the newcomer. *Gotta set things up for success*, she said to herself as she took things from a bag of purchases she had made at the animal shelter.

After storing away the cans of dog food, vitamins, food additives, protective devices against fleas and tick treatments, and a rubber chew toy, Amy took out the feeding dish and bed and placed them on the back porch. Meanwhile, Oshka had been excitedly cruising and sniffing the new environment. Amy sat down and started petting the pup lovingly. Gradually Oshka calmed down, wagging his tail, licking her hands, and showing all the natural affection of a little dog's heart.

Josh had been restless during the story reading. When it was concluded, he jumped out of Matt's lap and made for the kitchen repeating, "Oshka! Oshka!" He found his mom sitting on the floor holding the puppy in her lap.

"Come over here and sit down next to Mommy," Amy said. When Josh was seated, she said, "Now, watch what Mommy does." She gently stroked the little dog, running her hand smoothly over his back. Oshka's tail started flapping against the floor, and Josh's attention shifted. Amy imagined him thinking, *I'd like to grab that thing*. "Oshka does that to show he's happy," Amy said. She took his hand and, holding her own hand over it, guided Josh to gently feel the warm fur on the dog's back. "See how Oshka likes that?" she said. Josh smiled, his attention now on the pleasure of stroking the puppy. The dog turned his head and licked Josh's hand, and he drew back in surprise. "Oshka's giving Joshie a kiss!" Amy said in a reassuring tone.

After ten minutes of stroking, the puppy settled down sleepily. Josh's eyes were wide as he nodded. He had gotten the message. "I'm proud of you, honey," Amy said, hugging her boy. "Now, let's feed Oshka his dinner!"

Throughout the following weekend, Matt and Amy continued to work to emphasize gentle treatment of the new dog. They took Josh with them on short walks with Oshka leashed. They had many petting sessions.

Over the next two months, the parents were careful never to leave the puppy and child alone together. They purchased a kennel, which became Oshka's home base and comfort zone. By example and by word of mouth, they emphasized care and safety. They taught Josh to throw Oshka a chew toy but never to try to take it away from him. At the same time, they trained the puppy to be with Josh, and soon he was bringing the toy back and dropping it at Josh's feet for another throw. Amy always trained Oshka when Josh was present; for instance, they spent time training the puppy not to mind when his food bowl was picked up. Soon Josh was showing by his gentle actions that he loved Oshka, and the two were romping and playing together as fast friends.

PET CARE

Set things up for success

The choice of a pet should be appropriate to your child's age, size, and temperament. Study up on the habits of your new animal, including particulars of the breed for a dog or cat. Will the animal live mostly indoors or out-side? Will it have the run of the place? If not, what means can be used to establish its area? Parents should agree ahead of time on rules and guidelines for the new addition. As soon as possible, start teaching your child the value of ignoring poor pet behavior and praising good pet behavior.

Ignore failure and/or redirect

Even though it seems young pets and young children get along naturally, parents should not automatically expect kids and pets to interact appropriately. A pulled tail or ear can cause dogs in particular to associate pain with chil-dren and make them wary. During the first months a puppy is with you, never leave your child unattended with it. Most dog bites occur with children under the age of ten. Don't assume your child knows how to deal gently and protectively with animals. Communicate often with your child about the pet's needs, and teach him to observe the animal carefully. A rough or uncaring behavior from your child should be redirected. Demonstrate gentle treatment, let your child try it, and reward that.

Give a Whale Done!

As much as possible, be present when your child and pet are together, so that you can reward any instance of gentle caretaking and affection that is shown. Target specific behaviors and reward them immediately. Make each early playtime an opportunity for demonstrating the guidelines, having your child repeat the action, and then praising your child. Let your child know that you are proud of the progress he is making in caring for the pet. Help him feel pride in that accomplishment.

CHAPTER
Eleven

When Things Get Emotional
Time-outs

"**J**OSH. JOSH. *Joshie! Listen* to me!" Amy's voice grew louder, but it was no match for her son's voice, as the youngster wailed, screamed, and thrashed on the floor, beating his little feet against the carpet. His eyes were pinched shut, and tears streaked his fiery red face. Amy fell silent, suddenly realizing that with her insistence, she was only reinforcing Josh's poor behavior. He was having a full-fledged tantrum, and the longer Amy tried to reason with him, the louder and more upset he became. As she concentrated on calming herself, a scene came into her mind from a few days ago.

Amy and Kim Lee had been working with Kagan, a year-old killer whale, when the calf suddenly turned and swam away toward one of the underwater viewing ports that was being cleaned by a crew member. Kagan had been distracted by the sound of the squeegee rubbing on the window. When Kim Lee tried to get the whale's attention by slapping the water with her open hand, Kagan started to swim toward her, but at the last minute, he swung back in the direction of the glass. He even slapped his tail several times in an aggressive manner, letting Kim Lee know that he didn't want to cooperate. The whale was throwing a little tantrum.

Kim Lee tried calling him back one more time, but the whale totally ignored her, continuing to slap his tail flukes and pectoral fins so hard that he sent waves of water over the glass, drenching the unfortunate attendant.

"Let's go," Kim Lee said, walking away from the pool.

"Are we just going to quit working with Kagan?" Amy asked, puzzled.

"If he won't keep his mind on us," Kim Lee explained, "the wisest thing to do is leave the environment. Besides, he's very upset and not thinking right now."

"Give him a time-out, you mean," Amy said.

"Exactly. It's not only a time-out for the whale, but for us as well. We need to step back, try to think about why this happened, and plan how we'll proceed from here."

Clint had been observing the session. Now he came over and said, "You two did exactly the right thing to walk away from that situation. But you really had no choice at that point. My question to you is, what could you have done to avoid this problem?"

Kim Lee looked thoughtful. "We could arrange things with the crew member ahead of time, so he isn't cleaning the window of the pool where we're working with Kagan."

"Right," Clint said. "Eliminate the distraction before it happens. Not only was Kagan distracted for the training session, but he's very upset that you tried to divert him. You can see how one little mistake can lead to another—and even to aggression. It may take a little while now for him to calm down."

Now as Amy watched her young son carrying on, she thought about the day's events that had led to this hectic scene. She thought, *How could I have avoided this happening in the first place?*

Just then Matt came in the door. Taking in the scene, he asked, "What's got the little guy in such a snit?"

"I was just thinking about that," Amy replied, "although it's been kind of hard to hear myself think with this hullabaloo going on. Let's go somewhere quieter, and I'll tell you about it." They left Josh on the floor, still kicking and crying, and went to sit in the kitchen where they could observe him through the door. "Five minutes ago I was ready to pull my hair out," said Amy. "But I've been reviewing the day, and I think I have only myself to blame. It started when I overslept."

"But I woke you before I left for my early morning meeting," Matt said.

"I know, but I fell back to sleep," she admitted.

In fact, Amy had been rushing around, getting herself and Josh dressed and hurrying him through his breakfast. Amy had called to Josh repeatedly, insisting that he hurry. Meanwhile, Josh began resisting. He seemed to be purposely delaying things. Was he trying to make her angry? When she buttoned his shirt wrong, then impatiently jerked at it to start over, he scolded, "Mom-*mee*!"

She dashed to the car with him and hurriedly drove to the day care center. Josh's last look at her was a frown.

Her day at SeaWorld was hectic—and not much fun. Kim Lee, whose presence always calmed and reassured her, was out sick. It was cleaning day, never Amy's favorite thing. She had to work with fellow trainee Lorraine, who was in one of her moods. Then somehow time got away, and she was late picking up Josh on the way home. The little boy marched to the car without looking at her, and he was silent all the way to the grocery store where Amy stopped to pick up vegetables for dinner. Josh brightened a bit as he rode in the shopping cart, but then he began reaching for items, pulling things off the shelves. "No," Amy warned him. "Mommy's told you not to do that!" He kept it up. Once they were home, resentment toward his mother was percolating.

"Thinking back," Amy told Matt, "I know Josh was doing it because I wasn't paying attention to him. I was in a hurry to get out of the store and had other things on my mind. Also, he was really tired. So by the time we got home, it didn't take much to send our little anger astronaut into orbit. When I started cooking, he came in the kitchen and demanded we play with the puppy. I told him not now, we had to wait, and that did it. He started running around yelling, and finally just fell down and started screaming and going berserk."

Matt shook his head thoughtfully. "It was building up all day."

"Right," Amy said. "Guess I didn't set things up for success *this* time. My own attitude was so much a part of it. It's almost like Josh went into orbit because *I didn't*!"

Amy stopped, listening to the quiet that had settled over the living room. She jumped up and went to the door. "Josh, are you all calmed down now? Are you ready to come and play?"

"No!" came the angry reply. Then Josh began his wailing again, but this time only half-heartedly.

Amy shrugged and came back and sat down.

"Trying to catch the kid doing things right, were ya?" Matt said, smiling.

Amy rolled her eyes. "I thought he was done, but I guess not, so I'll let him sit a little longer. I just don't want to make the time-out longer than it needs to be. It can lose its effectiveness."

They waited a while longer. This time the noise subsided quickly.

Matt said, "I'll go."

"No way," Amy said. "This happened on my watch. I'm the one he's upset with. If you went in there, then you're the good guy. We don't want to get a good cop/bad cop thing going," This time when she went to Josh and said, "Ready, Joshie?" the little boy smiled and held out his arms.

Amy brought her son into the kitchen and sat silently with him. She and Matt wanted to make sure he was over his upset, so they gave him more time. After a minute or so, Amy said, "That's better now, isn't it Josh? You're all calmed down. How about a drink of water? You must be thirsty after all that fussing. Let's show Daddy the picture you drew at day care today." When Josh reached for a cracker and gratefully accepted a glass of water from Amy, it was obvious his episode was ended.

Turning to Matt, she said, "I learned one thing, and I should have known it from work, because the principle is the same with animals."

"What's that?"

"It doesn't pay to try to reason with an upset person. It's hard to try to make sense to an upset child—or for that matter, to an upset adult like a coworker or customer, or to a killer whale. It's best to just clear the area or do whatever is necessary to let the situation cool down."

"From what you told me," Matt said, "you're lucky Josh didn't decide to erupt while you were in the grocery store."

Amy nodded in agreement.

"So, what would you have done if it had happened there?" Matt persisted.

Amy thought a moment. "Ideally, if I'd kept my wits about me, I'd have left my groceries in the cart, picked him up and taken him to the car, and stayed with him until he calmed down. If he wouldn't calm down, I'd just have come home."

She looked at Josh. "Anyway," she said lovingly, "you and your mom certainly had a day of it, huh?" She hugged him tightly. "I love you, Josh," she said tenderly.

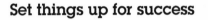

TIME-OUTS

Set things up for success

Time-out helps your child learn to accept responsibility for behaving in undesirable ways and, more importantly, for changing her own behavior. The time-out area should be easily accessible, where your child easily can be monitored while there. While in time-out, she should receive the least amount of reinforcement for a particular period of time. For young children, the time-out period should last only as long as it takes for the behavior to change. Communicate to your child exactly what the behaviors are that you want eliminated. Choose the time-out area, and eliminate toys and other distractions from that environment.

Ignore failure and/or redirect

When people (children or adults) are in an elevated state of emotion, it's useless to try to reason with them. While administering the time-out, you should define the specific behavior that resulted in taking this step. Short of imposing a time-out, the parent should use redirection. With younger children, this can take the form of distraction. With older kids, you can reason, perhaps saying, "I wasn't clear enough about this with you, I guess. Let's go over the rules again." Always try to end a redirection with a praising for something you "caught them doing right." Sometimes children misbehave in different environments where they think the home rules don't apply. If the upset happens in a public place and you have to leave, that small sacrifice can pay off later. When returning to the scene of the tantrum, you can work to get your child's agreement about carrying out the behavior you prefer.

Give a Whale Done!

As soon as the time-out is over, it's over. No grudges or recriminations. When you notice your child has elimi-nated the behavior that earned the time-out, be sure to call attention to it in a positive way. If appropriate, give praise for the fact that there have been no time-outs lately. You can always surprise a child in an unplanned way. ("You have been doing so well, Dad's going to take you out to your favorite restaurant.")

Potty Party
Potty Training

"**H**OW DO YOU get the most feared predator in the ocean to give you a urine sample?"

Amy, Lorraine, and Steve, SeaWorld's three new whale trainer trainees, looked at each other and shrugged.

Clint Jordan, who had asked the question, said, "Watch." Walking to the edge of the pool, he gestured to Kusti. Immediately the animal swam over to him. At his hand signal, Kusti hiked himself up onto the slide-out area where the water was only six inches deep . . . on his side!

Clint said, "We need urine samples on a monthly basis for each whale's health assessment. Before we trained the whales to give us a voluntary sample, it took a lot of time and effort to get one. We would have to drain the pool and put the whale on its side. Then the veterinarian would have to use a catheter—and a big one at that."

Everyone laughed.

"You can imagine how much the whales enjoyed that. Now all we have to do is what you're about to see. Today it's Kusti's turn," Clint said.

He gave the whale a few fish, then took a small cup and held it in front of the whale's eye. Going back to the genital area, he held the cup at the urinary opening. Unable to see what was happening, the others waited. Soon Clint gave a chirp on his whistle, straightened up, and the whale slid back into the water. After being rewarded with a fish treat for his good behavior, Kusti swam away. Clint held up the cup so that the audience could see the fluid level inside the backlit cup. The trainees let out a group "wow."

"That's amazing!" exclaimed Amy. Then she voiced the question that was in all three trainees' minds: "How'd you get Kusti to *do* that?"

Clint smiled. "As you look around, what would you say this pool is used for?"

Amy noted storage bins that held a variety of large toys and floats. She watched as one trainer tossed toys to a whale while two others gave a second whale a rubdown. "A playground pool for the whales when they're good?" she ventured.

Clint laughed. "We do in fact call it the Whale Spa," he said. "On the other hand, look over there." He pointed to a large mechanical device, saying, "That's our whale lift; it's especially designed for lifting a whale out of the water." He indicated the slide-out area he'd just used with Kusti. "So, can you guess now what this pool is really used for?" Getting no response, Clint explained, "This is where we give the animals shots, do blood tests on them, take urine and fecal samples from them, and sometimes drill their teeth if they have any damage or cavities." He paused to let that sink in. "Now, think about the human equivalent of these needs. Where do we humans go to have these things done?"

"A doctor's or dentist's office," came the replies.

"Right. And don't you all remember when you were kids and those were such fun places that you could hardly wait to visit?"

The trainees' responses were definite. "No way!" "You kidding me?"

Clint laughed again. "So, this is just repeating what you've already learned—that we always want these animals to learn that what we have to teach them is *fun*. If they don't see something as fun, exciting, enjoyable, or entertaining, they won't have much interest in it—especially if it hurts. Before we can get them to do what we want, we have to have their complete trust and confidence in us.

"With that as a basic principle, I'll answer Amy's question. In any procedure like this, it's important to set up the animal for success. In the case of training it to provide urine samples, that means catching the animal when it's likely to be relieving itself. By observing carefully, we've noticed that most whales, for whatever reason, urinate more in the morning.

"We had already trained Kusti to use the slide-out area. In this case, of course, we needed to teach him to slide out on his side, and that took some doing. Finally, he was able to do it. From then on, it was pretty straight-forward. I'd get him out, put the cup in front of his eye, and go back there and wait. Sometimes he'd pee a little, sometimes a lot, often not at all. I simply waited patiently, observed him a lot, gave him lots of attention—and of course a reward when he did pee—and none when he didn't. Finally, Kusti and I started getting all the steps together. It was about three months before it was going off without a hitch."

"It was incredible!" Amy said after telling her husband about Clint's demonstration of how to take a urine sample from a killer whale.

Matt shook his head.

"What's wrong?" Amy asked.

"I was just thinking," he said. "How is it they can get a killer whale to urinate on cue, and we can't get our son to pee into the toilet?"

Josh's potty training had indeed been a source of frustration for both parents. For now, they discussed the ten-day trip to New Mexico that Matt was about to take—the longest the couple were to be apart since their wedding. His job as chief computer programmer at his technical consulting company required him to teach classes around the country.

The next morning after they said good-bye, Amy was changing Josh's diaper. *Sopped as usual,* she thought to herself. Then the realization came: Typical of new parents struggling with a child's behavior, she and Matt had been going about potty training haphazardly. They had concentrated on getting the child's behavior changed, without thinking about what was in it for him. Now she decided to apply behavioral science principles. *Why didn't I think of this before? Wouldn't it be great if Josh and I could have this potty thing solved by the time Matt gets back?*

On her drive to Josh's day care center, Amy thought carefully about how to apply each step she was learning at SeaWorld. *I've already begun the most basic step,* she thought, *which is to observe Josh carefully. There are two areas in which I've got to start collecting data. The first is his urinating schedule. When is he most likely to wet his diapers? Is there a pattern?*

During the next few days, the young mother began experiments in giving Josh extra liquids and periodically checking to see the results. Next she needed to convince him that this project was fun. Which toys, songs, and activities were his favorites? Reflecting on whale-training precepts, she kept thinking, *Be positive, never calling attention to errors. Don't concentrate on results at first, only on building Josh's association of the toilet with fun. Be ready to praise progress at every opportunity.*

Occasionally she would think she was spending too much time on developing this approach. But then she thought, *What we were doing before sure wasn't working. It was driving everybody crazy! Besides, if I succeed in this area, I'll have the confidence to apply these techniques to virtually any area of my child's development.*

Meanwhile, Matt was traveling, spending several days in one place teaching a class, then moving on. On a plane headed for Albuquerque he happened to strike up a conversation with his seatmate, a man named Tony. Before long, the two men were exchanging notes about their children.

"Our Philip is seven," said Tony. "He's been pretty good up to now, but these days it seems I'm having to bear down on him more and more. The thing that bothers me the most is hearing him sass his mother. My parents would never stand for that, and I won't, either."

"So, how have you been 'bearing down' on him?" Matt asked.

"I take him over my knee. Couple of times I've given him a real thrashing."

Matt was thoughtful for a moment. "So, does that help?"

"Well, he sure doesn't sass her when I'm around anymore! Why, don't you spank your boy?"

"No, I don't," Matt said. Then, seeming to change the subject, he said, "By the way, have you ever been to SeaWorld?"

Tony beamed. "Sure. We've gone there several times. What a great place! We especially like the killer whale show."

Matt smiled. "Happens my wife is learning to be a killer whale trainer there. I mention it because she's brought home some techniques they use with the animals that we've been able to apply as parents."

Matt's new friend looked doubtful. "What do you mean?" he said. "Kids are pretty different from whales."

"They definitely are," Matt agreed. "But in one respect they're the same—they all want to know *what's in it for me?* The method they call Whale Done takes advantage of that." He went on to explain how he and Amy had been working to change themselves: observing Josh's behaviors, identifying the things he liked that could be used for reinforcement, and being clear on the outcomes they desired—all while ignoring or redirecting his negative behaviors. "I frankly didn't think it would work," he added. "But it's amazing the difference just *changing what you pay attention to* makes in the way a child behaves."

"So, let me get this straight. You just look the other way when he screws up?" Tony asked dubiously.

Matt shook his head. "Some things you plainly can't ignore. That's when you use what the trainers call *redirection*. In a small child it can amount to distracting him into doing something positive and then rewarding him. In an older boy I think it would take the form of talking in a calm, kind way about what you want him to do differently.

I know at work when I use redirection with a computer student, I try to take the blame for the problem myself. Maybe I'll say to the person, 'I guess I didn't explain clearly enough the procedure I want you to follow. Let's go over it again.' It seems to work well."

Tony soon went back to a book he was reading, but several times Matt noticed he was staring out the window in deep thought. When they landed and the two were preparing to disembark, Tony told Matt, "I've got to say, your talk about what you call the Whale Done approach has got me thinking about what I could do differently with my son. Food for thought. Thanks."

One evening soon after Matt's departure, Amy began a routine of giving her son more fluids like juice and water along with his meals and snacks. She brought a variety of his favorite games and a brand-new toy into the bathroom and arranged them so that Josh had to sit on his potty chair to enjoy them. She made no move to take his pants down, just to have him sit and listen while she read or played a game or otherwise entertained him. She knew that she had to make the whole experience a positive one from the very start.

The next day the first thing Josh said when she picked him up at day care was, "Potty." When they got home, Josh took his mother's hand and led her straight to the bathroom. *Aha*, she thought, *the bathroom has become a Josh Spa.* That evening, following the feeding of liquids

and waiting the twenty to thirty minutes she had determined was Josh's usual span before urinating, she took
down his pants while they were playing in the Josh Spa.
Nothing happened. However, as soon as he got off the
potty and got his diaper and pants back on, he wet the
diaper. At that point Josh made a face and said, "Yucky!"
He had learned the word from Amy because she would
say it when she changed his diaper. Amy merely smiled
and thought, *All I can do is ignore it.*

The episode was repeated later that evening after dinner. Amy played with Josh for a half hour while he was
on the potty. As soon as his pants were back on, he filled
his diaper—but this time it was "number two."

On the third day of their routine, for the first time
she heard her son urinating while he sat on the potty.
"Oh, honey!" she exclaimed in genuine delight, pointing
to the results. "Mommy is so proud of you!" She immediately grabbed some of Josh's favorite but rarely given
treat, M&M's, and gave them to him. She continued to
make a big deal celebrating the small but monumental
event. Josh was beaming from ear to ear as he turned
around, looked in the potty, and said, "Yucky!" Amy
laughed and hugged Josh, and they both said, "Yucky!"

Finally came the evening when Matt returned. As he and
Amy settled down to talk, Josh came up to Amy. Pulling
at his diaper, he repeated, "Potty." Then Amy was able
to show her surprised husband the progress she and Josh

had made. They went with the child to the bathroom and she removed his dry diaper. When Josh sat down on his potty seat and urinated, Matt's eyes got big. He clapped his hands and praised his son loudly, "Josh is a champion!"

Amy then told Matt about the routine she'd learned at SeaWorld, which she'd been using with Josh. Over the next few weeks and months, the parents collaborated in applying the techniques. There were occasional setbacks, which the couple would formerly have thought of as failures, but they totally ignored them. Meanwhile, they profusely praised each and every step Josh made toward using the potty on his own.

Gradually, more and more often, Josh began going to his little seat and urinating on his own. Soon Dad was demonstrating the stand-up routine at the big toilet to his son, and Josh was repeating the action at his potty chair. When the child began to do his stools in his little chair, Amy included the teaching of toilet flushing by making a ritual of pouring the contents of the potty chair into the large toilet and having Josh flush it.

One evening after Josh was in bed, Matt and Amy were relaxing. "Honey," Matt said, "I want to tell you how much I admire how you've stuck to using Whale Done with Josh. I've learned a lot about the techniques from you. Most of all, I've learned persistence!"

POTTY TRAINING

Set things up for success

Determine to make toilet training fun. Emphasize the positive. Observation and patience are the rules for deciding the best time to begin—which may not be when *you* are ready. For instance, if a child insists on tearing off his diaper, that may not be a reliable clue; not wearing a diaper could simply feel better. Above all, remember to follow the Whale Done guidelines: Observe your child to determine what combination of key variables—time, frequency, likes and dislikes, and so on—are likely to result in success. Know these things ahead of time; be aware of cues (holding crotch, tugging at diaper, etc.) that your child is uncomfortable.

Ignore failure and/or redirect

Without reacting or in any way assigning blame, use the opportunity to *redirect*—in other words, give the least amount of attention to the "accident" while pointing your child's attention in the direction of doing something positive. Never call attention to the behavior you want to see disappear. Never emphasize the negative. Instead, catch your child doing something right!

Give a Whale Done!

Don't miss a single opportunity to call attention to any behavior that points in the desired direction. Don't wait for perfection; instead, praise behavior that is *almost* right. Determine what means you will use to reward progress: verbal praise, sticker chart, certificates, time with special toys, favorite foods, and so forth. The key is to have a variety of rewards available so you don't have to go looking for them or thinking about what will work best at that time. You don't want to miss the opportunity by being late with the reward. You may not always be around to notice, but keep an eye out whenever you are with your child for opportunities to give a Whale Done! Don't fail to reinforce any word or action that indicates your child is "getting it."

CHAPTER
Thirteen

Please and Thank You
Moral Development

KNOWING THAT what people called "good manners" were simply ways of treating others with respect and kindness, Amy and Matt wanted to instill those attitudes early on in their child. Having observed other small children acting rudely, they decided it was time for Josh to learn politeness before a problem arose.

In discussing how best to teach the behaviors they wanted from him, they came up with a Whale Done way of practicing them. Matt said he wanted to be the point person, so that Saturday he and Josh sat down on the living room couch, and Matt set a bowl of Cheerios®—Josh's favorite cereal—on the coffee table.

"You and Daddy are going to play a game, okay?" Matt announced.

Josh nodded, eyeing the Cheerios hopefully.

"The game is called 'Please and Thank You.'" Matt took one of the Cheerios and held it up. "Can you say please?" he said. As Josh reached for the cereal, Matt continued to hold it out of his reach and repeated, "Say please."

This time Josh said, "Pease," while continuing to reaching for the Cheerio.

Matt gave it to him, verbally praising him at the same time, but he held Josh's hand before it could travel to his mouth and said, "Now can you say, 'Thank you'? Josh, say thank you, thaaank youuu."

Josh looked up and said, "Thank you."

Immediately Matt cheered and applauded, and gave Josh more of the treat. Matt and Josh repeated this scenario two more times; then Matt ended it by saying, "Josh, you are such a big boy, and Daddy loves you so much!"

Matt and Amy repeated this "game" over the next couple of days, interchanging the types of rewards and scenarios to keep it fun and interesting for Josh.

"You know," said Matt, "I think with your help I'm getting the hang of Whale Done parenting. I mean, saying please and thank you aren't things you teach a killer whale, but what you've shared with me about working with the animals and seeing the processes repeated again and again means I can use them in just about every area of being a dad."

"It's true," Amy agreed. "We don't teach killer whales to dress themselves, either, but that's the next area I'm going to tackle using the Whale Done approach with Josh."

Amy and Kim Lee were having lunch at a picnic table on the SeaWorld grounds. As they chatted about their roles as mothers, they watched three whales moving lazily about in a nearby pool. It appeared that two of the animals were not getting along.

"Doesn't it look to you like Sagu is bullying Kagan?" said Amy.

"I don't know what's going on," Kim Lee said, "but Sagu is definitely bumping Kagan a little more than playfully."

Suddenly there was a swirl of water, and a black form rushed over to the others. It was Taat. As he pushed between the two antagonists, they quickly turned and went their separate ways. "Hey," Amy yelled in excitement, jumping up. "Did you see that? Taat busted up the quarrel. That was heroic!"

"Looked like it," Kim Lee replied. "However, Taat is Kagan's mom, and she just didn't like Sagu bothering her calf."

Noting Amy's forlorn look, her coach added sympathetically, "I know. We humans would like to believe that there is more to animals' motivation than accessing resources for survival. Fact is, life in the wild remains simple and harsh. Certain animals possess intelligence, but basically food, sex, and social dominance are the motivators in their lives."

Kim Lee was thoughtful. "Like most mammals, whales possess a strong maternal instinct while raising their young. Also, when the killer whales are in the wild, they travel in hunting pods and exhibit certain teamwork tendencies. Sometimes you'll see a killer whale slide itself up on a beach or ice flow, grab a sea lion or penguin, and toss it to the other whales. This is all about survival techniques, not moral choices."

"Heck," Amy said, "the whales have taught me so much, I guess I hoped they could be my teachers even in the area of helping my child know right from wrong. I guess not." She shrugged. "But I'll tell you this; I'm not about to leave the moral side of my child's life to chance. There are so many toxic influences out there—drugs, violence, vulgarity, cheating, and just a general loss of respect—I think we're in a state of national emergency."

"You nailed it," Kim Lee declared.

Amy looked troubled. "I'm confused," she said. "Even though I want Josh to grow up with a deeply developed inner sense of right and wrong that will guide his moral choices his whole life, it's hard to know just how to go about teaching it. I want to be a parent who models it, rather than one who preaches it. But I'm just not sure how to think about it." She smiled at her coach. "*You're* the one with a graduate degree in child development. Any pointers?"

Kim Lee didn't hesitate. "You're talking about moral intelligence—the capacity to understand right from wrong, to have strong ethics and to act on them, to behave in a right and honorable way."

"How do you think this moral intelligence shows up in people?" Amy asked.

"Moral IQ shows up in traits like honesty and integrity, the ability to feel sympathy for others' pain, to keep from acting out unkind intentions, to control one's impulses and delay gratification; to treat others with respect, and to stand up against injustice."

"A tall order, even for adults," Amy said.

"*Especially* for adults."

"Helping kids build character seems more difficult today than it's ever been," said Amy. "But I think it's important to go up against the constant stream of vulgarity and violence, and do everything we can to help our kids stay on the path of goodness."

Kim Lee nodded and said, "In one of my graduate classes we focused on how to parent moral intelligence. Probably the strongest point was about the *power of expectations*. Expecting your kids to act morally is actually part of setting things up for success; it's ensuring that your own attitude is right as a parent. If you're all worried about your child doing wrong as he's growing up, you'll be reinforcing his tendency toward those negative behaviors without knowing it."

"Interesting," said Amy. "It's like my grandpa used to say: you always get what you're looking for."

"Interesting that you should say that, because it feeds into the second Whale Done principle: ignoring failure or redirecting. If you're looking for your child to do the right thing, and he does the wrong thing, you sit down with the child and reason out *why* the right behavior is desirable, emphasizing what's in it for him. In an instance of dishonesty you might say, 'If you tell the truth, your friends will always be able to trust you. If you don't, they won't.' Then finish the redirecting with an expression of confidence: 'Sometimes it's hard to be truthful, but I know you want to be a person others look up to. It will bring me a lot of joy to see you being honest in the future.'"

"That's good," Amy said. "I probably wouldn't use those words with Josh, because I think he's still a little too young for them, but I want to adopt that attitude with him. I've become a big believer in the power of Whale Done. I want to help my boy be good by praising and rewarding every instance where I see him being honest, kind, and generous. I already see those traits taking root in his nature, and it *does* bring me joy. I know that those are the character traits that will bring him happiness in the long run."

"I agree," said Kim Lee. "Over the years I've applied what I've learned at SeaWorld to my role as a mother, and the biggest learning I've had is to remember:

The key to developing confident, competent, caring kids is to catch them doing things right.

"That's what Whale Done Parenting is all about," said Amy with a smile.

MORAL DEVELOPMENT

Set things up for success

Moral intelligence is learned. Start developing it when your child is a toddler. The latest research on moral development finds that six-month-old babies are already responding to others' distress and acquiring the foundations for empathy.* Many parents mistakenly wait until their children are six or seven to cultivate their moral side. This delay only increases their potential for learning destructive negative habits that erode moral growth. Teach, model, inspire, and reinforce so your child can achieve the virtues of empathy, conscience, self-control, respect, kindness, tolerance, and fairness. Above all, be a moral example yourself.

Ignore failure and/or redirect

Parents who hold these traits as strong values can have a tendency to lecture or reprimand a child whose behavior shows a lack of them. Avoid this by remaining positive and patiently working toward developing the moral sense in

*Parts of this chapter are based on the book *Building Moral Intelligence*, by Michele Borba (Jossey-Bass, 2001).

your child. This is an area where redirection is essential. When observing an infraction, avoid the temptation to react on the spot. Choose a time when you and the child are calm. Communicate respect and understanding as you describe the behavior you saw without blame. Go over the rules again in a kind but firm manner. With older children, you can ask questions that enhance your child's moral reasoning: "How would you feel if someone treated you that way?" Then end with a good feeling by finding something to reward.

Give a Whale Done!

Expect your child to behave morally. Trust her to do so. Then be on the watch to catch her doing something morally right. Encourage every act of decency and caring. When it occurs, communicate the feeling "I knew you would do the right thing." As your child adds more virtues to her moral repertoire, celebrate each evidence of her potential for self-discipline, humility, courage, integrity, and altruism.

A Poolside Chat
Resources for Applying
Whale Done Principles

DELVING INTO greater detail, this section will help answer questions you may have about the Whale Done approach as you prepare to use it with your own children. While this book has focused mainly on young children, Whale Done also works with older children, including teenagers—and, indeed, with people of all ages—because the approach is based on universal principles of behavioral science. We realize we have covered only a few of the many typical issues parents face. However, if you have been reading between the lines, you realize that Whale Done is an approach that, used with skill, can be applied to virtually any parenting situation. So, whenever you are faced with a parenting issue, think, *What would a Whale Done Parent do?*

SET THINGS UP FOR SUCCESS

Part of setting things up for success is understanding the concepts that form the basis of the Whale Done method. Following are some definitions of terms used in the book.

Whale Done

A Whale Done is any positive response on the parent's part to a desirable behavior the child exhibits. It calls attention to doing right and reinforces that behavior. The response might be verbal, tactile (e.g., a pat or hug), or material (e.g., a treat, toy, or Whale Done sticker on a chart).

Redirection

Redirection is the response the Whale Done parent makes to a child's mistake or undesirable behavior. Instead of calling attention to the behavior, the parent guides the child's attention away from it, back toward something positive. Redirection can take several forms:

> *Distraction:* Redirection can take the form of distracting the child's attention. For example, if the child is singing at the top of his lungs while you have company, you might say, "I like to hear your songs, but please sing more quietly." After the child complies, thank him and say, "Look, I've got a coloring book

here that needs some coloring done in it. Let's do it together."

Return to the rules: Assuming verbal explanation is appropriate for the child's understanding, the parent might say, "Let's go over the reasons why we want to keep our voices down when other people are around."

Praising: Redirection is most successful when it results in the child's doing something that the parent can reinforce through praise, reward, or recognition. "Thank you for lowering your voice, honey. Mommy loves to hear you sing softly."

Positive Reinforcement

The Whale Done parent looks for opportunities to reinforce (support, strengthen, build up) a desirable behavior. Reinforcement can take a variety of forms:

Verbal—thanking, praising, using a loving tone of voice, using the child's favorite pet name, and so on

Tactile—hugging, patting on the back or arm, taking the child in your lap, and so forth

Rewards—treats, snacks, toys, special times

Variable Reinforcement

Using different forms of reinforcement, rather than the same one or two all the time, introduces an element of surprise and fun, and makes each experience fresh and new. Certain reinforcements may be more appropriate than others, given the particular situations.

Extinction Burst

Sometimes things get worse before they get better. Suppose a young child has tantrums when going to bed, and the parents pay a lot of attention to the problem, unknowingly reinforcing it. When the parents learn about Whale Done and stop providing attention to the child, the tantrums may worsen. This reaction is called an *extinction burst*, and it is actually the first sign that Whale Done is working. However, if the parents think that the new program of ignoring and redirecting is failing, and give in and provide reinforcement to the child, tantrums will probably increase. On the other hand, if they weather the storm and hold out, not reinforcing the negative but immediately reinforcing any positive change, the child will gradually respond favorably to the change.

Proactive Behavior Response Plan

1. Target desired behavior. Be very specific with the behavior you want to teach.
2. Communicate the desired behavior(s) to your child in an age-appropriate way.
3. Communicate with other caretakers (spouse, grandparents, babysitter), and plan together your reinforcers to set up your child for success.

4. Reinforce desired behavior. Using a variety of reinforcers and variable schedules of reinforcement has been proven to be more effective.
5. Develop a maintenance plan. Don't take good behavior for granted. Continue to reinforce the behavior on a variable schedule to maintain it in the future.

Most Common Mistakes

- Not paying enough attention to the desired behavior after you establish it. Remember to catch your child doing something right.
- Not using the right reinforcers to maintain the desired behavior. Every individual and every situation is unique.
- Not varying your reinforcers. By using a variety of reinforcers, you will strengthen the desired behavior.
- Inadvertently reinforcing negative behavior. Timing of the reinforcement is critical. Make sure that you are applying the reinforcers at the precise time your child exhibits the desired behavior. If you don't, you may be reinforcing behavior other than the target behavior.
- Not proactively reinforcing the desired behavior. Be sure that you and other caretakers all apply your maintenance plan.
- Not being consistent. Behaviors sometimes get worse before they get better depending on the intensity and frequency of the undesired behavior. Be patient.

- Making exceptions. Don't allow the undesirable behavior even one time, especially with younger children. Doing so causes confusion.
- Focusing too much attention on the undesired behaviors. Redirect and save all the attention for the corrected behavior. Give the least amount of redirection to accomplish your goal.
- Showing frustration while using the Whale Done approach. Sometimes this is the reaction (reinforcement) that the child is looking for. Negative responses end up reinforcing the behavior.
- Being too hard on yourself when you take a misstep. It's okay to make mistakes. Mistakes do not make you a bad parent; they provide opportunities to learn.

IGNORE FAILURE AND/OR REDIRECT

Every parent has to deal at times with the consequences of a child's behavior. You can't ignore offensive or dangerous actions. But such misguided actions can range from the child's humming distractingly to her breaking a vase during a loud temper tantrum. We never condone responding with anger, and we certainly abhor the idea of laying hands on the youngster out of anger, spanking (discussed later) or shaking the child.

There are three levels of responding to a child's unacceptable behavior:

1. *Ignore* it. If the action is merely annoying or something you can tolerate (perhaps a toddler's first use of a cuss word), you might just mentally dismiss it. You also might check yourself to make sure you are not the model for what the child is doing or saying.
2. *Redirect* it. In the case of a more serious or obvious misbehavior, you can redirect it. If the child is getting rambunctious to the point of disruption, ask him to quiet down. Once he does so, reinforce him with a Whale Done.
3. *Give a time-out.* When no other response has been effective, a time-out may be the choice—especially when the child is in an elevated state of emotion or otherwise out of control, and reasoning things with her is out of the question. For example, the child sees candy at home or in a store and wants it—and begins to cry or scream to get her way. Remember that if you have given in to this behavior before, you have only reinforced it, and therefore it will repeat itself, probably even getting worse. When you try to correct it, it will take longer. Remain patient.

More about Time-outs

The time-out gives the child an opportunity to calm down and to think about his behavior (and perhaps even redirect it himself). It's also a chance for the parent to become calm and think about what steps to take next, or to come to a deeper understanding of why the child is behaving this way just now. You may discover that you haven't been observing your child or paying attention to his needs, thereby contributing to the problem.

When you first place your child in the time-out environment (one in which he cannot play, hurt himself, or bother others), his behavior may worsen for a time. Ignore this, seeing it only as his attempt to provoke further reaction, and knowing that as long as emotions are elevated, no learning of the desired lesson can take place. Don't intervene until such actions stop, and wait until calmness and quiet—and a measure of cooperation on the child's part—have been achieved. When the child realizes that his own behavior determines how short or long the time-out is, he learns responsibility for his actions.

Spanking

Our audiences usually laugh when we say, "It's not a real good idea to punish a twelve-thousand-pound killer whale and then get in the water with him." The remark not only lightens up the room; it makes a point. Your child is far from the size of a whale, yet the consequences of physically punishing her can be similar: Anger. Bad feelings. Lingering resentment. Revenge. If reinforced, these feelings can seriously harm relationships.

Because many of today's parents endured spankings, shakings, or other forms of corporal punishment when they were children, and because spanking *seems* to be effective at times (i.e., it may curtail an undesirable behavior in the short run), there continues to be much discussion on this subject. We still hear the old saying "Spare the rod and spoil the child," as if the very age of the adage enshrines it in wisdom. Some adults might say, "I was spanked and I got over it," or "My dad whipped us, and it taught us respect." They forget that such action evoked fear—the fear of a smaller person toward a larger one. And if it did produce respect, it was likely not self-respect.

Punishment can be physical, or it can be verbal. (In *Whale Done! The Power of Positive Relationships*, we refer to a manager's negative response as a "gotcha.") Almost always, physical punishment comes out of a parent's anger. Often, both the child and the parent are out of control. Getting physical with the child is just a logical extension of yelling and screaming.

It takes little imagination to realize that a parent's laying hands on a child while angry lessens trust and damages the relationship. This is why we try always to avoid any negative reinforcement in training animals. But there is an even more important reason not to physically punish children. In the largest study of children's self-esteem ever conducted (by Stanley Coopersmith, 1967), thousands of British schoolteachers were asked to identify children of high self-esteem. Research on the lives and backgrounds of these children showed that high self-esteem was not linked to the income level or educational attainment of their parents, nor did it matter whether both parents were present in the home. Instead, four key factors were found to contribute to high levels of esteem in children:

> *Acceptance:* From birth, the child was accorded unconditional acceptance just as he was. He did not have to change or conform—or do anything at all— to earn this acceptance. He knew he was secure; he had a place.

> *Respect:* The child's body, living space, appearance, dress, possessions and, most important, ideas were respected. (This is the principal area that corporal punishment diminishes.)

> *Giving back:* High-esteem children were involved in frequent charitable actions. Giving to others was seen to contribute to their good feelings about themselves.

> *Parents' esteem:* Children who felt deeply and basically good about themselves lived in a high-esteem environment. One or both parents, or someone else of significance such as a grandparent, provided models of self-esteem.

The biggest argument against spanking is that *it disrespects the child.* Hitting a child does not show respect for the child's body, space, and personhood and therefore (especially if repeated often) stands a good chance of damaging the child's self-esteem. Children who are beaten, shaken, or otherwise abused have a hard time thinking of their bodies as absolutely their own or of their personhood as inviolable.

What goes around, comes around. Children who grow up in a home environment of disrespect are likely to disrespect others, both as children and as adults. So, whenever you are tempted to think that spanking or physical punishment is the way to go, stop, turn away, or go to another room. Take several deep breaths. And figure out another solution. You'll be glad you did.

GIVE A WHALE DONE!

Psychologists tell us that as much as 90 percent of what human beings do is dictated by habit. Of course, habits are not bad per se; in fact, they save us all kinds of time and energy. Just think what a bother it would be if we had to learn every morning all over again how to walk! But the same ease and efficiency that good habits bring make bad habits hard to change. If you assume for a moment that virtually everything we think, say, and do is not freely chosen but habit driven, you can realize how much easier it is to stay in our comfort zones.

In most cases, Whale Done parenting does call for a change in habits. Prior to a change in the parent's response to the child, a change in thinking is necessary. Shifting our mental patterns can be difficult, especially if the new way goes against the way we were raised, how we saw our friends being raised, or how other parents we know respond to their children. Even if you're convinced that Whale Done is a better way, the mental needle wants to stay in the groove of the old ways.

However, if you set a goal of becoming a Whale Done parent, the thing you can bet on is the results we have seen with the whales and our own children and grandchildren—the proven science behind these methods. This approach takes practice, but the more you do it, the better you get at it. Along the way, you can feel good about yourself for your efforts. Self-esteem, studies show, is one of the marks of a good parent.

So let's suppose you decide to take on the task of Whale Done parenting (a job that is never done), and having just begun your journey, you and your child have a run-in. This, of course, happens to the best of us, and you should never feel discouraged. What makes this incident different from other such times is what you do afterward, as you are recovering. You may feel angry, frustrated, hurt, or guilty, but as you give yourself some time to cool down and think about the episode, the nature of your reflection should be different. You can use the experience to further you on your way toward your Whale Done parenting goal. Ask yourself the following questions as you walk away from any confrontation with a child:

1. *Did I set things up for a successful outcome?* What did I do or fail to do that helped set up my child do what he did? Did I ensure my child's privacy during our disagreement to avoid embarrassment?

2. *Did I communicate effectively?* Or did I use anger, threats, or put-downs?
3. *Did I use redirection?* Did I bring the least amount of attention to the undesirable behavior or attitude, and the most amount of attention to what my child did right?
4. *Did I walk away building the relationship or diminishing it?*

Such guided introspection can be invaluable for checking up on yourself. Granted, it means putting yourself on the spot if one or more of your answers is *no*. But in such cases, you simply do what the old song says: pick yourself up, dust yourself off, and start all over again.

If both parents are present and equally resolved to implement the Whale Done approach, the process is much easier. If you're a single parent, enlist the help of a family member, another member of the household, or another parent with whom to form a learning buddy group. The important elements of working together are providing consistency to the child and feedback to each other. Most important of all is catching each other doing things right.

We hope this book's accounts of working with these remarkable animals remind you to have fun while loving your kids. The days can seem long, but the years are short. Don't take even the difficult times for granted, because before you know it, kids are grown and gone.

The Science behind the Whale Done Approach

This book brings to the parenting of children many behavioral principles and techniques that have succeeded spectacularly in training killer whales and other marine mammals, making it possible to work with these animals cooperatively. In fact, these principles and techniques have been so successful—even with the most feared predator in the ocean, the killer whale—that they have changed the entire field of marine mammal training. And they are now expanding to the training of many other animal groups, from other wild animals to domestic pets.

What has made these principles and techniques extraordinarily successful is that they are based on leading behavioral science research and universal discoveries about changing behavior. This research initially focused on changing human behavior—both child behavior and adult behavior—and it is very consistent with the knowledge about human behavior that Ken Blanchard draws on in his many books. For a good introduction to this behavioral science research, see Alan E. Kazdin, *Behavior Modification in Applied Settings*, sixth edition (Wadsworth, 2001).

Thad Lacinak, Chuck Tompkins, and their colleagues were the world's pioneers in applying this behavioral science research to revolutionize marine mammal training. They shared what they were learning and doing in many scientific papers and presentations, such as those listed here.

Today the work of advancing the application of behavioral science principles to the training of animals is being carried forward by many thousands of professionals around the world. This work can be found by going to the Web sites of three leading associations:

IMATA: The International Marine Animal Trainers' Association fosters communication, professionalism, and cooperation among those who serve marine mammal science through training, public display, research, husbandry, conservation, and education. www.imata.org

ABMA: The Animal Behavior Management Alliance seeks to provide the latest behavior management information and technology in order to encourage optimal behavior management paradigms for both captive and wild animals. www.theabma.org

AZA: Founded in 1924, the Association of Zoos and Aquariums is a nonprofit organization dedicated to the advancement of accredited zoos and aquariums in the areas of animal care, wildlife conservation, education, and science. www.aza.org

Further Reading

Andrews, J., M. Boos, O. Fad, T. Lacinak, and G. Young. "Elephant Management: Making the Change." Paper presented at the ABMA Conference, April 11, 2005.

Kuczaj, S. A., II, C. T. Lacinak, O. Fad, and C. Tompkins. 1998. "Why Do Environmental Enrichment Devices (EEDs) Become Less Enriching?" Page 167 in *Proceedings of the Third International Conference on Environmental Enrichment.*

Lacinak, C. T. "Advantages of Random and Interrupted Reinforcement with Pinnipeds." Paper presented at the annual meeting, International Marine Animal Trainers' Association, 1977.

———. "Proactive Aggression Reduction in a Zoological Environment." Paper presented at the annual meeting of the American Zoo and Aquarium Association, September 7–11, 2003.

Lacinak, C. T., and S. Kaczaj. "When Is Environmental Enrichment Most Effective?" Pages 32–35 in *Annual Conference Proceedings: The Animal Behavior Management Alliance, Tampa, FL, 23–28 February 2003.*

Lacinak, T., and C. Tompkins. "Whale Done Approach: Keys to Animal Training/People Training." Paper presented at the Association of Zoos and Aquariums Annual Conference, September 13–18, 2005.

Scarpuzzi, M. R., T. N. Turner, C. D. Tompkins, C. T. Lacinak, and S. A. Kuczaj. 1999. "The Use of the 'Least Reinforcing Scenario' in a Proactive Training Program." *Abstract,* 27th Annual Conference, International Marine Animal Trainers' Association, Chicago, December 6–10, 1999.

Turner, T. N., C. T. Lacinak, C. D. Tompkins, M. R. Scarpuzzi, and D. L. Force. "Husbandry Training at Sea World." *Abstract,* Annual Meeting, International Marine Animal Trainers' Association, 1991.

Yordi, R., and T. Lacinak. "Training Gray Wolves (*Canis lupus*) as Conservation Ambassadors at BGW." Paper presented at the North American Wolf Conference, April 23, 2007.

Acknowledgments

Ken

I would like to acknowledge Ted and Dorothy Blanchard, who got me started on the right foot. I believe they were Whale Done parents. I'd also like to acknowledge my partner, Margie Blanchard, who models everything we teach. I would also like to acknowledge my friend and in-house editor Martha Lawrence for her hard work in preparing the manuscript for publication. I also thank Steve Piersanti, president and publisher at Berrett-Koehler, for his openness to venture with us into this new subject area of parenting.

Thad

I would like to acknowledge my beautiful daughter Michele, her husband Matt, my son Philip, and their wonderful and loving mother Barbara, who utilized the Whale Done approach in raising both of them. This approach has now been passed down to our handsome grandson Joshua, who happens to be the inspiration for many of the examples in this book. Josh, you are the most precious gift to all of us.

Chuck

I would like to acknowledge my loving wife Kathy, whom I have been married to for twenty-eight years. She has been my guiding light and inspiration during my entire journey of Whale Done. Without her wonderful spirit and support, I would never have seen my potential or the impact I could have on this world. I would also like to recognize my sons, Cody and Jared, two beautiful souls who have blessed their parents with more than one can imagine.

Both of us, Chuck and Thad, thank all the colleagues we have worked with over the last thirty years, who have helped and inspired us to constantly make improvements in the way we teach and strive for better relationships with the animals and people we learn, teach, and work with every day.

Jim

Heartfelt thanks to Barbara Perman, PhD—best friend, partner, and coauthor with me of *No Ordinary Move: Relocating Your Aging Parents*—who continues to inspire, challenge, and uplift me to do my best. I also thank Martha Lawrence, The Ken Blanchard Companies editor, and Steve Piersanti, founder of Berrett-Koehler, whose tireless work on this manuscript has continuously improved it. To my matchless coach Shirley Anderson and to friends Ryan Hommel, Tani Cohen, and Uri Cohen, who support and encourage me in my craft, I am grateful. Lastly, I acknowledge the help and inspiration of my peerless guru, Paramahansa Yogananda, and the Self-Realization Fellowship line of gurus.

About the Authors

Authors from left to right, Thad Lacinak, Jim Ballard, Ken Blanchard, Chuck Tompkins

Ken Blanchard

Ken Blanchard has had an extraordinary impact on the day-to-day management of millions of people and thousands of companies. He is a prominent, gregarious, sought-after author, speaker, and consultant.

Ken is the coauthor of many best-selling books, including the international blockbuster *The One Minute Manager®* and such other best sellers as *Leadership and the One Minute Manager, Raving Fans, Gung Ho!, Empowerment Takes More Than a Minute, Whale Done!, Managing by Values, Full Steam Ahead, The Secret,* and *Know Can Do!* His books have combined sales of more than twenty million copies in more than thirty languages. In 2005, Ken was inducted into Amazon's Hall of Fame as one of the top twenty-five best-selling authors of all time. The College of Business at Grand Canyon University bears his name.

Ken serves as the chief spiritual officer of The Ken Blanchard Companies, an international management training and consulting firm that he and his wife, Dr. Marjorie Blanchard, founded in 1979. He is also coauthor of *Lead Like Jesus* and cofounder of Lead Like Jesus, a nonprofit organization dedicated to inspiring and equipping people to become servant leaders and lead like Jesus. Ken and Margie live in San Diego.

Thad Lacinak

Thad is founder and co-owner of a behavioral consulting company, Precision Behavior. He is a former partner and vice president of behavioral programs at Ocean Embassy, Inc. In this role, he participated in international project development and consulting and works to advance animal behavior modification techniques within the zoological community. Thad was also integral to the instructional division of the company, teaching positive reinforcement–based courses to both zoological and corporate clients.

Prior to joining Ocean Embassy, Thad retired from a thirty-five-year career at Busch Entertainment Corporation (BEC), as vice president and corporate curator of animal training, where he directed animal training and enrichment efforts at all U.S. SeaWorld and Busch Gardens Theme Parks. He oversaw and coordinated the efforts of over 450 animal trainers and keepers at these parks.

Thad was instrumental in developing SeaWorld's and Busch Gardens' industry-leading behavior and training techniques, husbandry procedures, and spectacular killer whale shows. He led the team that won the prestigious Thea Award from the Themed Entertainment Association in 2007 for the "Believe" killer whale show. In addition, he has won numerous awards for presentations and workshops at professional conferences.

Thad is a founding member and former president of the Animal Behavior Management Alliance as well as a former vice president of the International Marine Animal Trainers' Association. He is also a member of the Association of Zoos and Aquariums, the Society for Marine Mammalogy, and the Association for Behavior Analysis. Since coauthoring *Whale Done!* in 2001, Thad continues to present keynote speeches, seminars, and workshops globally to major corporations explaining the Whale Done process, vastly improving working relationships. He also conducts animal training seminars specializing in aggression, agility, obedience, and many other areas in the use of operant conditioning for behavior modification.

Thad may be booked for speaking engagements based on *Whale Done!* and *Whale Done Parenting.* He may also be contacted for specific topics such as team building, keys to positive leadership, and executive management. He resides in Orlando, Florida, and may be contacted for a keynote, seminar, workshop, or executive retreat at tlacinak@gmail.com.

Chuck Tompkins

Chuck is currently corporate curator of zoological operations for Busch Entertainment Corporation (BEC). His tenure spans more than three decades of service with BEC, much of that time served as vice president of animal training for SeaWorld Orlando.

Chuck has training experience with more than 100 species, including killer whales, dolphins, pinnipeds, primates, birds of prey, hoofed stock, and canines. He also is a Florida state-certified and federally permitted master falconer. Chuck has authored and coauthored more than a dozen peer-reviewed scientific papers on training and behavior modification and has been honored many times by the International Marine Animal Trainers' Association.

In 2001 Chuck coauthored a *New York Times* best seller, *Whale Done!,* with Ken Blanchard, Thad Lacinak, and Jim Ballard. He frequently presents keynote speeches nationally promoting the power of positive relationships at work and home.

Chuck holds professional memberships in the International Marine Animal Trainers' Association, the Association of Zoos and Aquariums, and the Animal Behavior Management Alliance. Chuck has served as the training advisor for Canine Companions for Independence (Florida Region), on the executive board for the Central Florida Blood Bank, the executive board for the Boys and Girls Club, and the executive board of the American Cancer Society.

Chuck resides in Windermere, Florida, with his wife Kathy, and two sons, Cody and Jared.

Jim Ballard

Jim Ballard spent ten years in schools as a teacher, guidance counselor, and principal, then another ten years conducting teacher training seminars in classroom management, team building, and affective curriculum. When he met Ken Blanchard in 1973, Jim moved into corporate training. As a consulting partner with The Ken Blanchard Companies, he designed and facilitated award-winning management courses and coauthored six books with Ken.

On his own Jim has published *What's the Rush?*, *Mind Like Water*, and *Little Wave and Old Swell: A Parable of Life and Its Passing*. His role in *Whale Done Parenting* has been to compile the stories and suggestions of his coauthors and work them into a parable. His writing focuses on the themes of positive relationships, change, and empowering people to deal with problems like information overload.

Jim is a life coach and president of LifeCrafters.com, an organization that assists people to discover and live out their stories. LifeCrafters also helps organizations to develop stories that capture and express their identity in short engaging tales to build loyalty with customers and employees. Visit www.myjimballard.com.

The Ken Blanchard Companies Services Available

The Ken Blanchard Companies® is a global leader in workplace learning, productivity, performance, and leadership effectiveness that is best known for its Situational Leadership® II program—the most widely taught leadership model in the world. Because of its ability to help people excel as self-leaders and as leaders of others, SLII® is embraced by Fortune 500 companies as well as mid- to small-size businesses, governments, and educational and nonprofit organizations.

Blanchard® programs, which are based on the evidence that people are the key to accomplishing strategic objectives and driving business results, develop excellence in leadership, teams, customer loyalty, change management, and performance improvement. The company's continual research points to best practices for workplace improvement, while its world-class trainers and coaches drive organizational and behavioral change at all levels and help people make the shift from learning to doing.

Leadership experts from The Ken Blanchard Companies are available for workshops and consulting, as well as keynote addresses on organizational development, workplace performance, and business trends.

Global Headquarters
The Ken Blanchard Companies
125 State Place
Escondido CA 92029
www.kenblanchard.com
1.800.728.6000 from the United States
1.760.489.5005 from anywhere

Keynote Speakers

Blanchard Keynote Speakers present enduring leadership insights to all types of management-related events, including corporate gatherings and celebrations, association conferences, sales meetings, industry conferences, and executive retreats. Our network of speaking professionals is among the best in the world at engaging audiences to new levels of commitment and enthusiasm.

Blanchard Speaker Topics Include:
- Coaching
- Customer Loyalty
- Employee Engagement

- Leadership
- Motivation and Inspiration
- Organizational Change
- Public Sector Leadership
- Team Building
- Women in Leadership

To book Ken Blanchard, Thad Lacinak, Chuck Tompkins, or another Blanchard keynote speaker for your next event, please call:

United States: 1.800.728.6052
United Kingdom: 1.44.1483.456300
Canada: 1.800.665.5023
International: 1.760.489.5005

Or visit **www.kenblanchard.com/speakers** to learn more and to book your speaker today.

Social Networking

Visit Blanchard on YouTube Watch thought leaders from The Ken Blanchard Companies in action. Link and subscribe to Blanchard's channel, and you'll receive updates as new videos are posted.

Join the Blanchard Fan Club on Facebook

Be part of our inner circle and link to Ken Blanchard at Facebook. Meet other fans of Ken and his books. Access videos and photos, and get invited to special events.

Join Conversations with Ken Blanchard

Blanchard's blog, HowWeLead.org, was created to inspire positive change. It is a public service site devoted to leadership topics that connect us all. Nonpartisan and secular, this site does not solicit or accept donations. It is a social network, where you will meet people who care deeply about responsible leadership. And it's a place where Ken Blanchard would like to hear your opinion.

Tools for Change

Visit kenblanchard.com and click on "Tools for Change" to learn about Workshops, Coaching Services, and Leadership Programs that will help your organization create lasting behavior changes that have a measurable impact.

Ken's Twitter Updates

Receive timely messages and thoughts from Ken. Find out the events he's attending and what's on his mind.

The Other SeaWorld

SeaWorld opened to the public in March 1964. In that inaugural year, a few hundred thousand visitors passed through its gates. But the park grew quickly from that modest beginning, and today SeaWorld—more accurately three SeaWorlds—play host to more than 13 million visitors a year. Virtually all of those guests will experience the thing SeaWorld is best known for: presentations that showcase the remarkable power, beauty, and intelligence of marine mammals. Most SeaWorld visitors, at least those who haven't yet read a Whale Done book, probably have only a vague sense of what is required to establish a relationship between human and animal that results in the remarkable variety of behaviors in SeaWorld's shows.

But if the fundamentals of animal training are unknown to our guests, so too is another aspect of SeaWorld: putting our hard-earned expertise in animal behavior, biology, and husbandry to use in helping animals outside our parks. In any given year, as many as 1,000 wild animals will be assisted by SeaWorld. Some, like an orphaned California gray whale calf rescued on a Los Angeles beach and raised to adulthood, receive international media attention. But others—a sea lion entangled in fishing gear, a pelican fouled with crude oil, a manatee gravely injured in a boat collision—are rescued, treated, and returned to the wild with little fanfare.

Animal rescue and rehabilitation is a central part of Sea-World's *other* mission. Our parks entertain and educate thousands of people each day, but we are equally committed to helping conserve wildlife and wild places, often thousands of miles away from our parks. Through our own efforts and our support for the not-for-profit Hubbs-SeaWorld Research Institute and the SeaWorld & Busch Gardens Conservation Fund, Busch Entertainment commits millions of dollars to conservation projects on every continent.

We strive to put smiles on the faces of every person who passes through the gates of a SeaWorld park. We also hope that each of those guests leaves with a keener appreciation and respect for not just the animals they've encountered at SeaWorld, but for every living thing.

About Berrett-Koehler Publishers

Berrett-Koehler is an independent publisher dedicated to an ambitious mission: Creating a World That Works for All.

We believe that to truly create a better world, action is needed at all levels — individual, organizational, and societal. At the individual level, our publications help people align their lives with their values and with their aspirations for a better world. At the organizational level, our publications promote progressive leadership and management practices, socially responsible approaches to business, and humane and effective organizations. At the societal level, our publications advance social and economic justice, shared prosperity, sustainability, and new solutions to national and global issues.

A major theme of our publications is "Opening Up New Space." They challenge conventional thinking, introduce new ideas, and foster positive change. Their common quest is changing the underlying beliefs, mindsets, and structures that keep generating the same cycles of problems, no matter who our leaders are or what improvement programs we adopt.

We strive to practice what we preach — to operate our publishing company in line with the ideas in our books. At the core of our approach is *stewardship*, which we define as a deep sense of responsibility to administer the company for the benefit of all of our "stakeholder" groups: authors, customers, employees, investors, service providers, and the communities and environment around us.

We are grateful to the thousands of readers, authors, and other friends of the company who consider themselves to be part of the "BK Community." We hope that you, too, will join us in our mission.

A BK Life Book

This book is part of our BK Life series. BK Life books change people's lives. They help individuals improve their lives in ways that are beneficial for the families, organizations, communities, nations, and world in which they live and work. To find out more, visit www.bk-life.com.

Be Connected

Visit Our Website

Go to www.bkconnection.com to read exclusive previews and excerpts of new books, find detailed information on all Berrett-Koehler titles and authors, browse subject-area libraries of books, and get special discounts.

Subscribe to Our Free E-Newsletter

Be the first to hear about new publications, special discount offers, exclusive articles, news about bestsellers, and more! Get on the list for our free e-newsletter by going to www.bkconnection.com.

Get Quantity Discounts

Berrett-Koehler books are available at quantity discounts for orders of ten or more copies. Please call us toll-free at (800) 929-2929 or email us at bkp.orders@aidcvt.com.

Host a Reading Group

For tips on how to form and carry on a book reading group in your workplace or community, see our website at www.bkconnection .com.

Join the BK Community

Thousands of readers of our books have become part of the "BK Community" by participating in events featuring our authors, reviewing draft manuscripts of forthcoming books, spreading the word about their favorite books, and supporting our publishing program in other ways. If you would like to join the BK Community, please contact us at bkcommunity@bkpub.com.